THE CANON

AND THE CURRICULA

A Study of Musicology and Ethnomusicology
Programs in America

THE CANON

AND THE CURRICULA

A Study of Musicology and Ethnomusicology
Programs in America

by E. Eugene Helm

PENDRAGON PRESS

STUYVESANT, NY

Pendragon Press Musicological Series

Aesthetics in Music
Annotated Reference Tools in Music
Dance and Music
Festchrift Series
Franz Liszt Study Series
French Opera in the 17th and 18th Centuries
Harmonologia: Studies in Music Theory
The Historical Harpsicord
The Julliard Performance Guides
Monographs in Musicology
Musical Life in 19th–Century France
The Complete Works of G.B. Pergolesi
Pergolesi Study Series/Studi Pergolesiani
The Sociology of Music
Studies in Central and Eastern European Music
Studies in Czech Music
Thematic Catalogues

Library of Congress Cataloging-in-Publication Data
Helm, E. Eugene.
     The canon and the curricula: a study of musicology and ethnomusicology
programs in America / by E. Eugene Helm.
          p.   cm. — (Pendragon Press musicological series)
     ISBN 0-945193-42-4
     1. Musicology—Study and teaching (Graduate)—United States. 2. Eth-
nomusicology—Study and teaching (Graduate)—United States.   I. Title. II. Series.
     ML3797.H485 1994
     780'.71'173—dc20   94-34571
                                                                  CIP
                                                                   MN

Copyright Pendragon Press 1994

Contents

LIBRARY
ALMA COLLEGE
ALMA, MICHIGAN

Conclusions: Where We Are Now

THE CANON AND THE CURRICULA

INTRODUCTION

This survey has three parts. The first part, Background, is not one more history of musicology;[1] it is a brief sketch of changes that seem to have been most important in influencing musicology curricula.

The changes have often been philosophically opposed, so that sketching them makes the sketcher sound wishy-washy, changing sides in every new paragraph. But objective sketching has to be the rule despite seeming contradictions, or else these pages will amount to a mere polemic.

The second part, Foreground, is a report on current musicology curricula in certain American universities.[2] Its organization follows the events of graduate-student life from admission to graduation. It is not an attempt to summarize everything said about every musicology program in every brochure or announcement. Instead, I have attempted to convey the essence of whatever messages these universities are sending to their prospective graduate students in musicology. This means that the reader seeking specific, up-to-date references to individual institutions will often have to study the individual publications. And where I may be mistaken about some detail of a program or

---

[1] The most useful history and description is still that presented in Frank Lloyd Harrison, Mantle Hood, and Claude V. Palisca, *Musicology*, one volume of *Humanistic Scholarship in America: The Princeton Series*, ed. by Richard Schlatter (Englewood Cliffs, N.J., 1963). Descriptions of what musicology ought to be in the modern sense begin about as far back as Friedrich Chrysander's preface to the first *Jahrbuch für musikalische Wissenschaft* (Leipzig, 1863). A superb view of musicology's accomplishments and a chronicle of its never-ceasing self-examination is found in the main text and cited sources of the 1980 article "Musicology" in *The New Grove Dictionary of Music and Musicians*; the article is by Vincent Duckles with Howard Mayer Brown, George J. Buelow, Mark Lindley, Lewis Lockwood, Milos Velimirović, and Ian D. Bent.

[2] Strictly speaking, 27 American and 2 Canadian: City University of New York, Graduate Center; Claremont Graduate School, Columbia, Harvard, Indiana University, New York University, Princeton, Stanford, State University of New York at Stony Brook; Universities of British Columbia, California at Berkeley, Chicago, Colorado, Illinois at Champaign-Urbana, Iowa, Kansas, Maryland, Michigan, North Carolina, North Texas, Pennsylvania, Southern California, Texas at Austin, Toronto, Washington, Wisconsin; Wesleyan of Connecticut, West Virginia University, Yale.

ignorant of an institution's most recent curriculum revisions, I hope such defects will not significantly alter the general picture.

The third part is limited to the few conclusions strong enough to leap out of my tall stack of historical accounts, university catalogues, abstracts of papers read at professional meetings, and essays on trends in the discipline.

BACKGROUND

What is the purpose of humanistic scholarship? What, in fact, does the humanist scholar do?

The job of the humanist scholar is to organize our huge inheritance of culture, to make the past available to the present, to make the whole of civilization available to men who necessarily live in one small corner for one little stretch of time, and finally to judge, as a critic, the actions of the present by the experience of the past.

The humanist's task is to clear away the obstacles to our understanding of the past, to make our whole cultural heritage — primitive, pre-Columbian, African, Asian, aboriginal, Near Eastern, classical, medieval, European, American, contemporary, and all the rest — accessible to us. He must sift the whole of man's culture again and again, reassessing, reinterpreting, rediscovering, translating into a modern idiom, making available the materials and the blueprints with which his contemporaries can build their own culture, bringing to the center of the stage that which a past generation has judged irrelevant but which is now again usable, sending into storage that which has become, for the moment, too familiar and too habitual to stir our imagination, preserving it for a posterity to which it will once more seem fresh.[3]

Restoration Has Become The Most Obvious Product Of Musicology

Decay and Restoration

The decay and restoration of all cultural goods is a normal and innocent part of our society rather than evidence of unjustified neglect at last remedied or distortion now atoned and insight finally gained. Everybody knows that, for better or worse, we live in an age of historicism, that restorations of all kinds are a fact of life, and that there must

[3]Richard Schlatter, General Editor, Foreword to *Musicology*, op. cit.

2

be some body of generalization we can make use of when we undertake a specialized restoration. Yet despite this common knowledge each restoration in the *arts*, like each return to some other ideal of the past, seems more often than not to be perceived as one of a kind, necessitating the continual re-invention of the wheel.

One generation perpetrates methods of restoration that are regarded by the next generation as half-hearted, misguided, or destructive. Leonardo's great mural of the Last Supper in a church in Milan was only about a century and a half old when, in 1656, the friars living in the church enlarged a doorway to the kitchen by cutting through the legs of the Apostles. Since then at least seven major attempts have been made to restore the painting, but the first six attempts have been more like renovation (retouching, repainting, remaking) than restoration. Only since 1980 have restorers pursued the goal of removing all evidence of previous attempts at restoration and preserving what is left. Many astonishing details have emerged. Now we need to revise the reproductions and reconstructions and imitations of this painting that we have seen all our lives, such as the one in Forest Lawn cemetery in California, or the one in a wax museum in Fort Worth.[4]

Probably well over half of the classical music heard today (I use the common dictionary definition of ("classical") has had to go through the hands of restorers. The patent example is of course the music of J.S. Bach—forgotten in the second half of the eighteenth century, restored once in the second half of the nineteenth, restored again in the second half of the twentieth. Nineteenth- and early-twentieth-century editions of early music were often distorted by Romantic inflation and inappropriate applications of the doctrine of progress. Now, in the present age of historicism ("historicism" is a fairly new term, like "cultural relativism"), we make a special point of looking at music of the past in some approximation of its own terms. The good side of all this might be described as the revelation of past greatness. The bad side is that we might be too smugly unforgiving of inflations and adaptations— which, after all, are a tribute to the artworks involved, in that they seek to incorporate the past into the living artistic practice of the present.

It is, in fact, impossible to say whether the supposedly ever-more-faithful restoration of the arts and artifacts of the past is good or bad. I

[4]See, e.g., Herbert Kupferberg, "How You Can Help Save the Last Supper," *Parade*, Aug. 8, 1982, pp. 4-5.

do not share Allan Bloom's belief that it symptomizes the continued tragic decline of the unfettered, irrational, creative, Rousseauist-Nietzschean side of human nature.[5]

I believe the opposite: that if the Renaissance and the Enlightenment were almost as much a result of the restoration of decayed cultural goods as they were a result of new knowledge, and if they absolutely defined the mind of the West as distinct from the mind of the rest of humankind, then they are the paradigm for those cultural restorations large and small, old and not-so-old, that have been an increasing part of Western civilization for the last four or five centuries. Restoration side by side with the genuinely, scientifically new is a mainstream broad and deep. It can neither be curtailed nor increased by fastening upon some superficial manifestation of it and describing it on that false basis, nor by setting up and knocking down whatever straw men happen to be most closely related to it at present. It is misleading, for instance, to speak of early-music performance in general or the increasing use of early instruments in particular as a passing phenomenon, as some kind of blip in the history of music, or to manufacture conflicts between so-called antiquarians and so called mainstream musicians, or, on the other hand, to impose a deadly sense of spirit-killing obeisance unto the god of authenticity.

The exquisite complexity of cultural restoration, mainly a product of Western culture, came out of the arrival of literacy in the West. Literacy separates the West from much of the rest of the world. Being able to write and read weakens our short-term memories and strengthens our long-term memories. The opposite is true in non-literate, or oral, cultures. In the non-literate culture the bard or the tribal elder has a short-term memory that is phenomenal by Western standards; he must carry what history he knows in his head. If he fails to transmit the tribal epic to younger heads, an important part of tradition is lost forever. In the West, on the other hand, once something is written down it can be safely forgotten, at least for awhile. It might be a musical score, play, poem, architectural plan, novel, treatise—or, just as important, a dusty but somehow preserved manuscript dealing with sculpture, painting, history, philosophy, aesthetics, politics, religion. As long as an undercurrent of oral transmission accompanies that document on the library shelf, the document can be more or less faithfully interpreted, provided that familiarity with documents of that kind has not yet bred contempt

[5]In *The Closing of the American Mind* (New York, 1987).

for their conventions. But then too much time passes, too much water flows under the bridge. The innocent and unavoidable process of neglect sets in. Eventually some remembered remnant, some thread of repute leads someone to pick up the document once again. It is now nearly indecipherable, or—what amounts to the same thing—the norms of interpretation attached to it have been largely forgotten. The restorer has his work cut out for him. He has to pay the price for our collective literacy. He must put to the test our notion that anything written down is recoverable.

Rich and powerful societies are usually literate societies. They lead the way in the preservation and restoration of not only their own cultural goods, but—in their own terms and under their own conditions—even the cultural goods of societies less rich and powerful. The world's greatest museum of African art is not in Africa but on the Mall in Washington, D.C. Indonesian graduate students come to American universities to study Indonesian music. The Pergamum Altar and the bust of Queen Nefertiti are in Berlin. The Elgin Marbles and many of the treasures of King Tutankhamen are in London. The Winged Victory of Samothrace and the Venus of Milo are in Paris. All this plundering took place in the name of preservation. When Lord Elgin's agents erected scaffolding around the Parthenon at the beginning of the nineteenth century, chiseled off the frieze chunk by chunk, and shipped the chunks to his estate in Scotland to serve as decoration (until their eventual removal to the British Museum in London), they were not really resisted by the natives. To the occupying Turks the beautiful sculptures were blasphemous and suitable only for target practice, like the Sphinx in Egypt; to the native Greeks, the Parthenon sculptures were invisible.[6]

Yet even in societies that are only partly literate, scales do eventually fall from eyes, and the fever of restoration takes hold, influenced by national pride and apparently in direct proportion to the degree of literacy in the population. Now the Egyptians are trying to save the Sphinx. A piece of the Sphinx's beard is in a back room of—where else?—the British Museum, and the director of the Egyptian Antiquities Organization wants it back. Until her recent death, Melina Mercouri, the Greek film star who became Minister of Greek Culture, continued to negotiate through UNESCO for the return of the Elgin Marbles to the Acropolis.

[6]See, e.g., Russell Chamberlin, *Loot! The Heritage of Plunder* (New York, 1983).

Related to these examples is the growing esteem in the West for almost any kind of *easily understood* restoration. Hard-bitten editors of important but obscure documents wish they could tap some of the enthusiasm and insight lavished upon the restoration of an old sailing ship by the citizens of Galveston (with less interest in the ship herself than the values and crafts associated with her), or a carousel in Colorado (with absolute insistence on following original craft techniques), or the Jenny airplane (repenting of the use, at first, of modern materials and finally demanding completely original materials), or—to carry these examples to a logical extreme—the Duesenberg automobile once owned by the actor Tyrone Power (repenting of the wrong kind of paint and having to remove it before the authenticity-obsessed restorer could begin). These may be trivialities, but they demonstrate that, increasingly, the well-conceived and easily understandable restoration project can do no wrong in the eyes of its public. More than that, they show that the idea of restoration which began in the Renaissance, with all its false starts, circuitous paths, and dead ends, is still a fundamental part of our society.

* * *

For some time now, as I have said, most classical music has been handed to the public by scholars mining and restoring the music of the past: musicians of various stripes, among whom musicologists have accomplished, and increasingly accomplish, the most consequential work of restoration. Few performers of classical music in concerts, broadcasts and recordings find their main repertory in the new, relying instead on editions of past music often made available by musicologists. It is primarily musicologists who have provided a vast literature on the restoration of past performance practices. Yet more fundamental than systems of editing or styles of performance has been the basic *discovery* by musicologists of what some classical-music radio stations call the ever-growing repertory of music of the past. And most worthwhile critical discussion of classical music—analysis, valuation, biography, history—originates either with musicologists per se or with theorists, composers, critics, or performers whose entire outlook is colored by two centuries of musicological inquiry.

Living in a musical museum

It seems a remarkable and disturbing thing to say: old music now outweighs new music by a considerable margin in the lives of classical musicians and in the hearts and minds of their audiences. One theory has it that such historicism is a sign of our century's musical sterility. Adherents of this idea point to the contrast between our meek deference to the past (as in the much-debated quest for "authenticity") and the attitude of Renaissance restorers, who typically felt free to reshape their restorations of the treasures of Antiquity according to their own creative whim.[7] The quest for "authenticity" in restoring music from the remote past is seen by some as a confession not only of present-day artistic bankruptcy but as a sign of actual contempt for the living traditions that connect us with our musical inheritance; putting old and exotic music into the sealed display case of authenticity, carefully removing the taint of all those corrupting but altogether humane traditions that connect past and present time, has the eventual result of separating us from that music rather than linking us with it.

Other misgivings: our appreciation of unique masterpieces fades as the second-rate is given equal billing. We may buy more records of newly resurrected compositions for the sake of novelty, but the demise of one serious music publication after another and the financial crises of one orchestra or opera company after another show how superficial is our actual dedication to the traditional institutions of classical music. The keen edge of our creativity as composers is blunted by our fear that at this late date there may be nothing new under the sun. Or we present early music side by side with avant-garde music and non-Western music because in their arresting strangeness these presentations distract us from the fundamental anomie and emptiness of our own musical lives. Or, shaking off the crushing weight of our whole "cultural inheritance," we deconstruct it all, abandoning "elite" standards of valuation in favor of multiculturalism and gender equality. Meanwhile, the young seem to feel nothing but indifference toward any classical music.

Building anew on our inheritance

Opposing these apocalyptic views is the cheerful observation that musicians have always been molded by the past—meaning centuries ago or yesterday—and that we now have easy access as never before to incalculable riches, a hoard of art that cannot fail to inspire us to new levels of creativity.

---

[7]A very good survey of the outlooks of Renaissance restorers is included, along with an encyclopedic view of cultural restoration in general, in David Lowenthal's *The Past is a Foreign Country* (Cambridge, 1985).

Just as writers depend on past writings, and painters, sculptors and architects depend on past visual arts, composers can build the new only on a foundation of the old. The masterpieces of twentieth-century composition, at least as numerous as masterpieces from any other period, are more identifiably descended from inherited compositions than ever before, as much by reaction as by imitation. Preserving, restoring, building on the past is the essence of Western civilization. The juggernaut of restoration will not be stopped, whether the object being restored is the Egyptian Sphinx, the Sistine Chapel ceiling, or a 1957 Chevy. Restoration today is as much worth the trouble as it was when Erasmus endorsed it nearly five centuries ago: "To restore great things is sometimes not only a harder but a nobler task than to have introduced them."[8] And when a cultural inheritance is destroyed, as in Nazi Germany or the Chinese Cultural Revolution or the Cambodian genocide or the Somali famine, apocalypse becomes a reality rather than a literary conceit.

Musical restorations have filled our libraries

Whether the vast corpus of inherited music is stultifying or stimulating, whether contemporary music would have taken a different turn without so much restoration everywhere, whether historicism simply joins impressionism, serialism, neoclassicism, and all the other isms of twentieth-century music as a value-neutral fact, nobody can yet tell, despite the extensive literature on the subject; because the present scale of musical restoration is unprecedented in the entire history of music.

Unprecedented, but not unexpected. The restoration of past cultural goods, and the synthesis of the inherited with the newly created, has characterized the West since the Renaissance. In a society whose culture is embodied in written records much more than in oral tradition, including a thousand years of musical notation, it is only natural that libraries should fill up and that their contents should become increasingly the concern of scholars. From the Renaissance to the present, from the invention of printing to the invention of desk-top publishing, in music as in literature, architecture, and the other arts, monkish devotion to collection and preservation has been increasingly supplemented by scholarly attempts at restoration. With the passing of the

---

[8] In a letter of 1516 to Leo X, letter 384, *Correspondence*, 3: 221-2, quoted by David Lowenthal in *The Past is a Foreign Country*, op. cit., p. 84.

eighteenth-century Enlightenment attitude that today's arts are superior to yesterday's, and in the fever of Romantic attachment to the past, modern musicology was born. By the middle of the nineteenth century, restorations of past music reached their first flood. Scholars like Philipp Spitta and Friedrich Chrysander could refer for the first time to modern editions or modern studies of Dufay, Ockeghem, Josquin, Willaert, Palestrina, Giovanni Gabrieli. The first complete Bach and Handel editions began to appear, and these led the way for the rapid discovery of Schütz, Buxtehude, Lasso. Scholarly restorations of Gregorian chant were begun by the Benedictine monks of Solesmes. The Romantic "addition of strangeness to beauty" extended not only to the remote past but also to remote cultures, to the global perspective of a new discipline, ethnomusicology. A new availability of old and exotic music, along with a dawning idea that art should be evaluated as much as possible in the terms of its own time and place, made it necessary for musicographers like Kiesewetter, Fétis, Winterfeld, Ambros, Spitta and Chrysander to reinterpret the work of such eighteenth-century scholars as Burney, Hawkins, Martini, Gerbert, and Forkel.

Making sense of overflowing bookshelves

The stage was set for an attempt to bring the new body of knowledge, the new understanding of distant greatness, into more comprehensible order. This new systematization is only about a century old. It was given the title *Musikwissenschaft* (translated not quite accurately as "musicology"). The classic early outline of the field appeared in 1885 with the founding of the *Vierteljahrsschrift für Musikwissenschaft* by Spitta, Chrysander, and their younger colleague Guido Adler. The lead article of the first issue of that journal, written by Adler, is entitled "Umfang, Methode und Ziel der Musikwissenschaft." In its enormous influence on later generations, it constitutes the first graduate musicology curriculum.

Adler's scheme has its roots in outlines of musical knowledge going at least as far back as the seventeenth and eighteenth centuries; he continued to revise it for most of his career. It is also one product of the fervid infatuation with scientific method that took hold of many a discipline in the second half of the nineteenth century. It seemed more obvious then than it does now that the humanities might rival the stunning achievements of science by adopting some of its organizational apparatus—taxonomy, for instance. Here is a condensed version of Adler's taxonomy of *Musikwissenschaft*:

I. Historical: epochs, places, peoples, individuals, etc.

   A. Early notations

   B. Musical Forms

   C. Laws

      1. As exemplified in compositions

      2. As propounded by theorists

      3. In artistic practice

   D. Instruments

(Auxiliary sciences: history, paleography, chronology, diplomatic, bibliography, library and archive science, literary history, languages, liturgical history, history of mime and dance, biography, statistics of institutions and performances, etc.)

II. Systematic

   A. Harmony, rhythm, melody

   B. Aesthetics, psychology

   C. Music education

   D. Ethnomusicology

(Auxiliary sciences: acoustics, mathematics, physiology, psychology, logic, grammar, metrics, poetics, education, aesthetics, etc.)

One wonders what went through Adler's mind when he made what today looks like a ridiculous list of the "auxiliary sciences" of musicology. If this was a way of getting a foot in the door for the new discipline, it succeeded, for Adlerian musicology, in both its historical and its systematic branches, became the primary training ground for musicologists from the beginning to the middle of the twentieth century, crossing the Atlantic to America from the decade before World War II through the decade after. But along the way it lost much of its phantom apparatus under the rising tide of *old music newly heard.* What lasted was Adler's vision of the musical work of art itself as the starting point of musical scholarship. It was the pursuit of this vision by his innumerable disciples that caused some of the pigeonholes of his plan to remain empty while others filled to overflowing. Paleography and restoration, historical style criticism, ethnomusicology, biography, general history—these became the main ingredients of the musicology curriculum, not because statistics, logic, physiology, psychology and all the rest are any less worthy of study "for their own sake"—the motto of science—but because a lifetime of scholarly devotion is not long enough to concentrate solely on the musical work of art itself and the circumstances that created it. Meanwhile, each of Adler's "auxiliary sciences" has developed in its own right beyond all imagining, approachable by the non-specialist only in the most amateurish way.

It is *heard music* that has constituted musicology's most obvious contribution. I use the value-neutral word "obvious" with care. Musicology can be proud of transforming the lives of the great and the less great, inside and outside the professional music world, by the simple expedient of exposing them to past genius. Yet it would be a cheap definition of music that allowed it to be only an immediate gratification, ignoring the age-old question of what music is, expressing little curiosity about why, among all God's creatures, only *homo sapiens* is concerned with music. From the writings of Ancient Greek philosophers to the present, knowledge about music (which is what the term "musicology" was coined to mean a century ago) has continued to claim vast tracts in astonishingly diverse fields—no doubt in justification of the dignity and importance of such study. But it must be admitted that some of these claims have been made in self-defense, to present an impressive front, especially in the early years of the discipline, when many opponents of musicology found it hard to wrap their minds around the concept of a *métier* whose practitioners were primarily neither performers nor composers. The reported reaction of President A.L. Lowell of Harvard to the new word "musicology" was typical of the liberally educated generalist who instinctively rejects jargon: "Nonsense—the word doesn't exist. You might as well speak of grandmotherology."[9]

For Lowell as for other academics it was frivolous to give a name to and impose a formal structure upon a realm of knowledge so general as to be amorphous, one that had largely been pursued by the merely erudite (usually philologists and their ilk rather than professional musicians). In Lowell's time, up to 1933, Harvard's department of music majored in composition; not until after World War II did scholars come to dominate the musical scene there. *Webster's New International Dictionary* has defined musicology only since 1934. And musicology has gained a foothold in the university only in recent times. The first American Ph.D. in musicology was J. Murray Barbour at Cornell in

[9] Harrison, Hood, and Palisca, *Musicology*, op. cit., p. 141.

1932. The founders of the *Vierteljahrsschrift* and other early builders of complicated musicological taxonomies obviously anticipated such difficulties. They realized that the new discipline would have to be launched with enough momentum to breach a solid wall of suspicion and indifference. Their way of accomplishing this was characteristic of the zealous founders of many a newly named field of scholarship: to build a theoretical framework impressive in its intricacy and seriousness.

In 1915 Waldo S. Pratt imitated, for Americans, Adler's groundbreaking of thirty years earlier by inaugurating the first issue of *The Musical Quarterly* with a famous article entitled "On Behalf of Musicology." Here Pratt reviewed some earlier classifications of musical knowledge. He found Adler's outline too typical of "German encyclopaedic categories," "more practically serviceable than theoretically satisfying." Another formulation, that of Hugo Riemann around 1908, had five main divisions: acoustics, tone-physiology and tone-psychology, musical aesthetics, theory of composition, and music history. Riemann's plan, said Pratt, "leaves out too much, and confuses logical categories." But Pratt never questioned the idea that musicology must be "scientific," and he went on to propound his own system, one that turned out to have very little lasting effect on American musicology. Most of his categories—"metrics," "rhythmics," "mechanics," "psychics," "technics," "practics," and the like—have just sat there on the fringe while the Bach revival, the Handel expansion, the Vivaldi discovery, the whole early-music movement and similar restorations have galloped along, spurred by a revolution in mass communication the foreknowledge of which would have sent the astounded Adler, Riemann, and Pratt back to their drawing boards. In their generation scholarly editions of music were still considered primarily monuments—*Denkmäler*—rather than fodder for performers. But mass communication, including not only the broadcast media and recordings but also microforms, photocopy machines, desktop publishing, computerization, and easy access to the sources, has changed everything. We still treasure the hernia-inducing *Denkmäler* as avenues to understanding, but now they serve too as sources of heard music.

The creation of theoretical machinery some of which is destined only to rust is, as I have said, not surprising; it is a standard and innocent feature of the establishment of a new discipline. Even as late as 1941 it still seemed logical to some of the best American minds to regard the increasing availability of music not previously heard for centuries as relatively unimportant to the core of musicology, and to repeat the catechism of scientific musicology—paradoxically without being very much influenced by the most recent accomplishments of science and technology in making great music actually heard. Glen Haydon's *Introduction to Musicology* of 1941 certainly influenced a whole generation of American musicologists, particularly in lending dignity to a profession widely besieged and little understood, but neither that generation nor any since has practiced what Haydon preached. His book is an inch thick. About three-quarters of an inch is devoted to elementary acoustics, physiology and psychology, aesthetics, "the theory of music theory," pedagogy, and ethnomusicology. A quarter of an inch goes to historical musicology. Since long before 1941 the real engines of musicology have been music history and ethnomusicology, both of which, like art history, include "everything," starting with the work of art itself and gradually discovering the surroundings, not so much by the application of science per se but by means of procedures related to science, methods that have come to be grouped under the term "scholarly rigor." Today we can say that Haydon's emphasis was in the wrong place.

The definition stabilizes

Ever since World War II the old descriptions of musicology offered by Adler, Riemann, Pratt, Haydon and their contemporaries have sounded not merely outdated but almost like wishful thinking. The facts of musicological experience, as opposed to theoretical constructs, do not seem to have been reflected in descriptions of musicology much before 1957, the year of Manfred Bukofzer's monograph *The Place of Musicology in American Institutions of Higher Learning*. Bukofzer unceremoniously categorized such subjects as acoustics ("the science of meaningless sound"), physiology, and psychology as "independent fields in the natural or social sciences, rather than the humanities. According to an old and by now outdated classification these fields are said to belong to 'systematic musicology'; actually they are fields auxiliary to musicology proper . . . ."[10]

In 1963 a new survey of the field appeared, the abovementioned *Musicology*, by Harrison, Hood, and Palisca. With the chapter of that book entitled "American Scholarship in Western Music," Claude Palisca inaugurated a series of observations on musicological trends that, to American musicologists at least, confirm the validity of what they themselves have

[10]pp. 42, 45.

13

actually accomplished and what they hope to accomplish.[11] Palisca pointed out the longstanding primacy of a musicological mainstream in America: music history and ethnomusicology. He mentioned the misgivings of such figures as Charles Seeger, Oliver Strunk, R.D. Welch, and Curt Sachs over some of the "scientific" classifications current in their time. He gave full credit to the Haydon textbook for its influence, but noted the "tacit admission by the author that acoustics, physiology, psychology, and aesthetics may be preparatory to musicological work but are not really part of it."[12] Palisca observed that disciplines "outside the fields of historical and ethnological musicology"[13] were very much neglected between 1950 and 1960 in the *Journal of the American Musicological Society* and *The Musical Quarterly*, as well as in graduate musicology programs during about the same period. Since 1960 such journals as *JAMS, MQ*, and *Ethnomusicology* have continued in this vein; so have the papers read at local and national meetings of the American Musicological Society and the Society for Ethnomusicology.[14] The basic picture Palisca drew in the early sixties had changed by the early eighties, he says, only in "the intensified and more critical exploitation of some traditional ways of doing scholarship,"[15] and still seems familiar in the nineties:

> Specifications for subjects in which the Ph. D. may be taken typically state that it may be in theory, musicology, or music education. A closer look at a university catalog usually reveals that the courses in musicology are actually in the history of music, though occasional introductions crop up in the aesthetics of music, folk music, primitive music, or Asiatic music. Acoustics appears rarely, and the courses in psychology of music that are encountered seem to be destined for students in music education.
>
> The evidence, whether it is the consensus among active musicologists, the material published by scholarly reviews, or the

---

[11]Palisca has continued his discussion of the discipline in the section on music in Part 2, Volume I of the UNESCO study *Main Trends of Research in the Social and Human Sciences*, The Hague, Paris, New York, written in the early 1970s but not published until 1978, reprinted as "Reflections on Musical Scholarship in the 1960s," along with a new editor's introduction by Palisca, in *Musicology in the 1980s: Methods, Goals, Opportunities*, ed. by D. Kern Holoman and Claude V. Palisca (New York, 1982).

[12]p. 99.

[13]Ibid.

[14]Except perhaps for the remarkable 1990 joint meeting of AMS, SEM, and the Society for Music Theory in Oakland, California; see p. 27 below.

[15]Editor's introduction, *Musicology in the 1980s*, p. 12.

programs of university music departments, points to a conception of the field in America that is far more specific than that of its European founders. The acoustics, psychology, physiology, and pedagogy of music have become truly peripheral areas that musical scholars prefer to leave to specialists outside of music. Theory is usually left to composer-teachers and aesthetics to philosophers.

* * *

Caught up in the enthusiasm for scientific discovery even historians in the middle of the nineteenth century embraced science and claimed to be engaged in it. Once history was part of science, it was easy to annex to musicology both true sciences like acoustics and pseudo-sciences like pedagogy, musical sociology, and anthropology, and to consider them all scientific disciplines. While we are ready to acknowledge the benefits of the methodological purge that the scientific movement incited, today we no longer deceive ourselves about the scientific status of history.

There remains the most cogent reason for eliminating scientific subdisciplines from musicology. If musicology is to have any standing among the liberal disciplines, it must meet the standards of humanistic scholarship. These standards are as rigorous as those of science, but are distinct from them. What the controlled experiment is to science, the authenticated document or artifact is to musical scholarship. Just as science is not limited to evidence gathered from experiments, but exploits carefully measured and recorded observations of natural phenomena, so the musicologist uses living samples of music making faithfully recorded and observed. Written documents, including music; pictorial or sculptural representations; musical instruments; and other remains constitute the principal forms of evidence used by the historian. Live music making, data gathered from living informants, and musical instruments are types of evidence most fruitful for the ethnomusicologist. But both historical and ethnical musicologists use all of these types of evidence, and the two fields overlap at many points.

* * *

The area of the musicologist is, then, distinct from the areas of the theorist, the acoustician, the aesthetician, the psychologist, and the pedagogue. *The musicologist is concerned with music that exists, whether as an oral or a written tradition, and with everything that can shed light on its human context.*[16]

If the curricula surveyed in Part II of this study still generally support the fundamental outlook presented by Palisca over three decades ago, that

[16]Palisca, in *Musicology*, op. cit., pp. 100-101, 105-6, 116.

is hardly an indication of unanimity as to what musicology *should* be. The issues continue to be broad and deep, as is attested in nearly every musicologically or ethnomusicologically oriented journal or meeting, and in the following pages. "Music in the life of man" vs. the written-down music of an elite; the "ethnomusicology of Western music"; overspecialization resulting in isolation; overgeneralization resulting in cheapening; comparative musicology vs. musical anthropology; positivism vs. criticism; theory as part of musicology (as in Germany) or as distinct from it (as in the U.S. and Britain); theory and analysis in present-day music; the information explosion and the computer; iconography; links between musicology and music education—these and many other issues will no doubt keep the conversation going into the indefinite future.

The persistence of systematic musicology

It would be both unjust and inaccurate to underestimate the continuing importance, in some distinguished musicology programs,[17] of studies in such fields as acoustics, physiology, psychology, and aesthetics, still generally grouped under the rubric of systematic musicology. Furthermore, there is nothing particularly fixed in the scope of systematic musicology; today it includes research techniques, liturgiology, philology, church history, and aspects of theory and ethnomusicology, topics that are to be found in many a university curriculum. One has to take these curricula very seriously indeed if the program is as distinguished as that at, say, the University of Hamburg, or if the aura of real scientific procedure, in addition to the scholarly rigor now expected in all the humanities, seems to surround outstanding programs like that at the University of Pennsylvania (see pages 58–59). These programs look back on the rich philosophical history of music since Antiquity, a history treasured and jealously guarded by every serious musician. None of us wants to give up our intellectual connections with the Quadrivium. That alone is reason enough to think twice before discarding any aspect of systematic musicology in favor of making more music heard. I would rather read a fine dissertation on the musical and philosophical background of Kepler's cosmological theories in the seventeenth century than hear another note of Michel-Richard de Lalande's insipid *Sinfonies pour les soupers du Roi*, from the same century.

---

[17]Mostly outside the U.S., at institutes of musicology in such places as Hamburg, Cologne, Berlin, Warsaw, Lubljana, Moscow, and Tokyo, according to Palisca in "Reflections," op. cit., p. 16.

Still, out there is the overwhelming presence of musical restoration accomplished mostly by musicologists, and it seems perverse not to acknowledge that presence publicly and noisily as the most *obvious* (that value-neutral word again) product of musicology in the first century of its formal existence.

Ignoring the obvious

No such acknowledgement has been forthcoming. The music-loving public remains generally baffled by musicology and isolated from it, partly because musicologists from Arnold Schering through Manfred Bukofzer to Joseph Kerman have regarded the mere resuscitation of old music as one of the incidental functions of the discipline. A long succession of presidents of the American Musicological Society have complained about the separation of musicology from the public. The *Grove* article on musicology contains the familiar lament that "American musicology has barely breached the long-established barriers that divide the forces of serious intellectual life from the vast media that produce and disseminate music."[18] Restoration goes on apace but audiences know nothing of it. Too many scholarly papers seem to be addressed to a handful of specialists and nobody else. New Ph.Ds in musicology go jobless while radio stations specializing in classical music employ untutored announcers, because musicology Ph.Ds would not be caught dead in such positions. Similar academic isolation and snobbery keeps these Ph.Ds out of publishing, journalism, commerce, arts management, recording companies. Music education would achieve a new validity if musicologists could somehow be inspired to find a better way of sharing their grasp of music literature with the young—although it may well be that this battle was lost long ago. Public schools long accustomed to giving their students Shakespeare and Dickens, or at least aspiring to bestow such gifts, remain hostile environments for Purcell and Brahms. The National Endowment for the Humanities keeps on singing the old refrain about the divorce of university humanities departments from the taxpayers who support them. Surely one way to help close the breach between musicology and the public—a breach that would be even wider if it were not for all that music heard consensually—would be to point out and take pride in musicology's contribution to the standard repertory.

But we hesitate. Bringing old music back to life does not seem to require as much mental ammunition as certain specialized pursuits that

---

[18]Op. cit.

cannot be easily explained to a mere music lover. Not wanting to be classified as ordinary mechanics, musical scholars cannot read this statement by Bukofzer without second thoughts on the topic of editing:

> An immense amount of . . . [musical] knowledge can be turned directly to practical purposes, but the utilitarian point of view is neither the sole nor necessarily the driving aim of the musicologist. It would betray a very limited conception of musicology if it were thought of only as the willing handmaid of musical practice supplying fodder for the concert hall. . . . The discovery and revival of old music is a genuine and very important function of musicology, but it is not the only one.[19]

On the other hand, few musicologists are unaffected even now by Arnold Dolmetsch's famous outburst at the beginning of the early music revival:

> Will this [old] music ever be heard again? Will music, like the sister arts, ever retake possession of its past, its heirlooms, its rightful inheritance? Yes, it must; and by patiently working backwards, mastering each step, the now dim past of music will be brought to life, and will take its place side by side with the other arts, to which it never was inferior. But it is not through the deadly kind of research in which the Germans have led the way that any advance will be made. Is it worth while to devote years of labour to compile an exhaustive list of all the operas and other compositions that were performed at some German Court during two or three centuries, with the names and particulars of all the composers, singers, musicians, dancers, copyists, &c., engaged there, and the dates of their entering and leaving the service, and their salaries &c., when not a single phrase of any of the music can be correctly heard? What avails it to know when the grandfather's uncle of a certain lutenist was baptized, or how many wives he had, if neither the lutenist's music nor a lute is procurable?[20]

Today the opposing views of Bukofzer and Dolmetsch are neatly perpetuated in two recent books on musicology: Denis Stevens's *Musicology: A Practical Guide* (New York, 1980) and Joseph Kerman's *Contemplating Music: Challenges to Musicology* (Cambridge, Massachusetts, 1985). Stevens shows his British training and his long experience in creating musical programs for the BBC by his flat-footed emphasis on what he calls "applied musicology," meaning musicology devoted to restoration and performance.

---

[19]*The Place of Musicology,* op. cit., p. 26.

[20]Arnold Dolmetsch, *The Interpretation of the Music of the XVII and XVIII Centuries Revealed by Contemporary Evidence* (London, 1916, reprinted 1946), p. 468.

Kerman, on the contrary, is at great pains to align himself with the German tradition in his comments on the Stevens book:

> This thoroughly blinkered view of the topic would have made even Thurston Dart blush. One would never learn from Stevens — who has also written numerous articles and books on medieval English polyphony, Monteverdi, and other subjects — that musicology is seriously implicated with the history of music, that history has merit in itself, or that history has anything to do with criticism. Yet there is something seductive, too, about this vision of the applicability of scholarship to the non-scholarly world. Probably more than a few musicologists have greeted this self-announced "practical guide" to their discipline with a twinge of instinctive sympathy. As for people outside the discipline, the only reason most of them pay musicology any heed is because it unearths music they can hear in concerts and on records.[21]

Indeed, asks the layman, if restoration is not primarily what you practice, what *do* you do? A simple answer would show more strength than a smoke screen of incomprehensible terms or a pseudo-literary essay devoted to dropping the greatest possible number of vogue-names per page. One could answer that musicology is simple, that it has only two parts: restoration and understanding. All the musicological activities that culminate today in the preponderance of old over new in heard classical music are elements of restoration; all critical, theoretical, ethnomusicological, philosophical investigations of music that have occupied noble minds for many centuries are elements of understanding. It is astonishing that my neighbor, a distinguished microbiologist and connoisseur of classical music, does not know this. If the occasion ever arises, I will put aside all reservations and explanations and say to him, "The core of your record collection has been handed to you by musicologists." Once he understands how that came about, and what the performers named in the liner notes owe to musicology, he will give credit where credit is due, smilingly admitting that he thought musicologists only pursued minutiae. Then I will seize the advantage and add, "and much serious thinking about music—writing its history, or asking what it really is, or explaining why some of it is so highly valued—is also the business of musicology and theory. Musicologists and theorists, after all, are the authors of the really important books and articles on music that line the shelves of the local public library." Here he will not follow me as far, since his musical interest lies more in hearing

[21]p. 182.

music than in talking or reading about it; and in any case I would not want to push him into the devastating layman's comment that words about music always seem to mean less than the music does.

More criticism and less positivism?

Only time can tell whether what is most obvious (that word again) will also turn out the be most valuable in musicology curricula. When Carlyle wrote the phrase now chiseled into the façade of more than one library, "In books lies the soul of the whole past time," he probably would have agreed also that our inheritance of a tangible, concrete—obvious—body of art created centuries ago or yesterday is the beginning and end of our apprehension of art. Yet is the mere unprecedented accessibility of virtually "the whole past time" in music sufficient cause for the establishment of new syntheses, a further recasting of the scholarly study of music? Is the irresistible march of performers into musicological precincts—more evident each year at meetings of the American Musicological Society and the Society for Ethnomusicology—a symptom of a fundamental alteration of the nature of musical scholarship?

Again, this is a survey, not a polemic. But surely scholars do not believe that the inner meaning of music is always best approached through writing about it rather than listening to it. It is a cliché to say so, but the opposite is more often the case. Which means that the most mundane product of positivistic musicology, namely, editing, can be the most efficacious way of perceiving the secrets of music. Even so, no sane musicologist wants to give up thinking about, talking about, writing about music simply because he or she has had a hand in making an edition of it, bringing it to performance, putting it on the music stand. One might argue that it is time for musicological positivism to retreat into the background now that so much of our musical heritage is immediately available to us, while musical criticism comes at last into its own. Joseph Kerman's much-discussed call[22] for the establishment of serious music criticism in the place of much positivistic musicology, not the usual journalistic criticism and not the usual level of analysis but "the study of meaning and value in art works,"[23] has to be earnestly considered. Without such consideration the work of musical restorers is not

---

[22]Dating back to a long debate in *Journal of the American Musicological Society* with Edward Lowinsky during 1965 and brought up to date in *Contemplating Music*, op. cit.

[23]*Contemplating Music*, op. cit., p. 16.

worth the candle. Without such criticism many a composer will be disinterred who should remain buried.

True and false criticism

Music criticism should close the notorious gap that has separated it from literary and art criticism since the time of Jacob Burckhardt and Heinrich Wölfflin. A critic in the highest sense is one who ranges over the art works of all periods, making distinctions between treasure and trash without apology, justifying those distinctions, and thus helping to enclose "the best that has been thought and said" in a protective web of words that reach back through centuries of tradition. How ironic, then, that much new criticism calls itself criticism at all. It seeks not to identify the good but to call into question, on political or social rather than aesthetic grounds, the very aesthetic judgments that define our civilization. Real criticism, the kind Kerman apparently wants musicologists to do, might well be the only possible antidote in music to this new kind of criticism. It might be the only remedy for the cultural relativism that is rapidly eroding the idea of an artistic canon as part of this culture's essence. Our music history textbooks still describe a musical canon. This canon is more easily heard than ever before. But reverence for it, emotional involvement in it, and any deep understanding of it are rapidly passing under wave after wave of different cultural possibilities and different standards of value.

I tell an ethnomusicologist colleague that my highest duty as a teacher is to transmit the three B's to young people; he answers that such an ambition is fine as long as I realize that the three B's occupy a place not much higher in the young person's scale of values than does, say, Tibetan chant. He is also likely to say that true criticism, true assessment of value, cannot begin with a foregone conclusion about the worthiness of any canon. We bring up that possibility and several others in the next section.

A final point

But first we must conclude this discussion of restoration with one more comment. The great body of restored compositions newly heard, the plain *existence* of this body as it continues to mold the whole shape and character of classical music, casts into relative invisibility all words written *about* music. It is easy to see, generations later, how truly insignificant were most words written about music when such words were intended specifically to fill some sterile pigeonhole in the musicological taxonomies of an Adler or a Pratt. Closer to home, we have higher hopes for our own debates about positivism vs. criticism, or "political correctness," or new musicological paradigms derived from literary studies,[24] as well we should, because this time we are informed by history rather than by the fashion of the moment. We have to believe that we are now escaping the danger of false paths, that our own words about music will turn out to be less doctrinaire and therefore more universally applicable than was the pseudo-science of an earlier musicological era (even when, in the current aping of literary criticism, our words are tortuously and comically contrived to include the obligatory references to Foucault, Derrida, de Man, Lacan, etc.). We can only insist that the long traditions of musicography and music history and music theory— as old as civilization—have always been essential, integral, defining aspects of the musical art itself, often at the highest creative level. But the fact remains that words about music will *forever* be secondary to the unstatable import of music itself. We musicologists know this perfectly well—don't we? Uncertain as to the value of words about music, we should be reassured concerning the work we have done to bring actual music to the music stand. We should declare proudly that in most of our musical restorations we have accomplished something unquestionably significant and enduring. If we do not make that declaration, we are selling our discipline short.

Musicology And Ethnomusicology
Are Not Yet Integrated

Surely most historical musicologists are by now among the converted who acknowledge that ethnomusicology in arly any of its main guises is a richly rewarding discipline worthy of representation in nearly any graduate musicology curriculum. If the average historical musicologist seems indifferent as to whether an ethnomusicologist colleague belongs, say, to the Merriam or Hood camp, perhaps that is because scholars have more interest in a fellow scholar's intellectual caliber than in his or her party affiliation. They are glad enough to have the field of ethnomusicology well represented, and they are willing to negotiate the details. Where curriculum is concerned, the details should reflect,

---

[24]As discussed by Joseph Kerman, for instance, in the Spring 1991 *Journal of Musicology*.

within limits imposed by the whole musicology faculty, the particular interests of the ethnomusicologists on that faculty.

Shall we, then, study music "in culture"? Yes. Or shall we understand music "in terms of itself" and also "in society"? Yes. Shall we understand it partly by means of instruction in non-Western performance? There is still no clear answer, even though, as discussed below, American *historical* musicology has turned out to be neither willing nor able to cut itself off from performance. The best-laid curricula in such a young and vital discipline as ethnomusicology are bound to change as drastically as the broad musicology curriculum has changed during the past century. The vast literature of ethnomusicology's self-examination, its enormous effort of definition and redefinition, seems to go on unabated. That should hardly surprise us as we ride the rollercoaster of worldwide political, economic, and ethnic revolution.

Ethnocentrism vs. cultural relativism

Among the current issues of ethnomusicology that seem most perturbing to planners of graduate musicology curricula—and, indeed, to university faculties everywhere in every branch of the humanities—is the question of balancing the ethnocentrism that is part of every individual culture against the cultural relativism that is primarily an attribute of the West. Stanford University, for instance, revised its basic undergraduate curriculum a few years ago to delete or de-emphasize some of the classics of Western literature, art, and philosophy in favor of works from the Third World, from non-Western sources, from a greater number of women (such as the diary of a Guatemalan socialist and feminist revolutionary as a replacement of Dante's *Divine Comedy*). This brought on a nationwide flurry of outraged editorializing and academic alarums, along with second thoughts at Stanford, to the effect that our students need to absorb their own cultural inheritance, which is contained in a relatively few works that happen to be elitist and male-oriented, before they can even attempt to understand the minor works of their own culture or any important aspect of other cultures, that they must be molded by the idiosyncrasies of their own civilization before they can perform humane actions on the world stage, and that a strong sense of self-identity and self-worth is indispensable in a chaotic world. Allan Bloom's recent book *The Closing of the American Mind*[25]

[25]Op. cit.

joins this chorus on behalf of the Western classics, persuasively enough to make the book a best-seller by academic standards; but it and similar polemics[26] have been attacked on practically every American university campus for allegedly demonstrating a narrow and selfish view of a world desperate for cross-cultural understanding.

A surprisingly powerful phalanx has formed among the professoriate in the humanities, a movement born in the counter-culture of the sixties and dedicated, in the name of justice, equality, and anti-authoritarianism, to the partial or total dismantling of the Western cultural canon. Little understood off the campus, this movement unites postmodernists, deconstructionists, and post-structuralists in literary and art criticism; feminists; racial and sexual minorities; Third-World revolutionaries; scholars and practitioners of non-Western art, music, philosophy, literature, religion; and Marxists whose ideas about proletarian art (including the crudest and meanest rock and rap) seem to be spreading as rapidly as political Marxism is collapsing. A few years ago it seemed that the core of the Western musical heritage could not possibly be subjected to the same kind of reassessment that has allowed academics to declare many a literary classic essentially meaningless on the ground that its purpose was only the manipulation of one class of society by another (i.e., the white Euro-centered male). But now just such a reassessment is being carried out within the field of musicology on many important fronts.[27] Who can argue with such happenings? Who cares to question the aspirations of the deprived and the oppressed around the world? Who wants to knuckle under to the so-called wisdom embodied in the so-called canon?

---

[26]For instance, Roger Kimball's *Tenured Radicals: How Politics Has Corrupted Our Higher Education* (New York, 1990); Charles J. Sykes's *The Hollow Men: Politics and Corruption in Higher Education* (Washington, D.C., 1990); various speeches by former Secretary of Education William Bennett; various publications by the National Endowment for the Humanities.

[27]See, for example, Rose Rosengard Subotnick's essay "Musicology and Criticism" in *Musicology in the 1980s*, op. cit., in which musicologists are taken to task for accepting the validity of any writing about the meaning or value of any music--e.g.: "Interpretation today, I believe, is largely an individualistic activity because it takes place in a world that no longer provides rational support for beliefs in any single set of principles, values, or conceptions of truth as a basis for universal understanding of one, single, unmistakable meaning" (p. 147). The whole essay is a plea for musicologists to join the mainstream of modern literary and art criticism, but apparently only under the banner of post-structuralism.

More to the present point would be such questions as these: Is it possible that certain art works endure because they really are superior, regardless of the gender, race, or class of their creators? Is political probity a criterion of great music? Is some music within a given tradition better than other music within that tradition? Is it worthwhile to try to determine what makes one art work better than another? Is there any danger in considering anybody's handiwork to be just as good as anybody else's? Is art worth pursuing for its own sake? What was Oscar Wilde driving at when he said "All art is quite useless"?

Cultural relativism and the ethnomusicology curriculum

It amounts to a paradox, and not a simple one. But now let us narrow the discussion to the ethnomusicology curriculum. Where ethnomusicology is concerned, the paradox takes on a special force in the Bloom book:

> A very great narrowness is not incompatible with the health of an individual or a people, whereas with great openness it is hard to avoid decomposition. The firm binding of the good with one's own, the refusal to see a distinction between the two, a vision of the cosmos that has a special place for one's people, seem to be conditions of culture. This is what really follows from the study of non-Western cultures proposed for undergraduates. It points them back to passionate attachment to their own and away from the science which liberates them from it. Science now appears as a threat to culture and a dangerous uprooting charm. In short, they are lost in a no-man's land between the goodness of knowing and the goodness of culture, where they have been placed by their teachers. . . . Science's latest attempts to grasp the human situation—cultural relativism, historicism, the fact-value distinction—are the suicide of science. . . . Cultural relativism succeeds in destroying the West's universal or intellectually imperialistic claims, leaving it to be just another culture. So there is equality in the republic of cultures. Unfortunately the West is defined by its need for justification of its ways or values, by its need for discovery of nature, by its need for philosophy and science. This is its cultural imperative. Deprived of that, it will collapse.[28]

What compounds the paradox is that here Bloom is pointing to the most precious object of the ethnomusicologist's attention: the non-Western musician's traditional immersion in his own "vision of the

---

[28]Bloom, op. cit., pp. 37-9.

cosmos," so that other such visions are subsumed into his own rather than being set aside as isolated, scientifically collected specimens. Implicit in the Western ethnomusicologist's view of that music, then—Bloom would say—is a schizophrenic denial of the self-sufficiency, the self-justification, of his own culture while necessarily imputing just such self-sufficiency to the musical culture being studied. If he truly holds to this view, the ethnomusicologist is cutting himself off from his own people, hoping forlornly that he will be adopted by aliens, taking a desperate chance of being abandoned, suitcase in hand, on the station platform. I meet rootless students every semester who seem dedicated to taking that chance, students who have never been intoxicated on even one occasion by any aspect of their own musical heritage. But—third stage of the paradox—suppose one answers that the genius of Western culture (as opposed to that of other cultures) is, or is becoming, not so much a rejoicing in its own idiosyncrasies as its ability to compile a magisterial understanding of individual cultures around the world, and their interrelations. Bloom might observe that such a view presupposes a colossal, final contempt, a contempt that may be conscious or subconscious, for every one of the individual cultures or societies being studied, since each of these charming, worthy, enlightening bodies of culture is destined to become a mere molecule in the vast structure of Western scholarship. No wonder ethnomusicologists, anthropologists, folklorists are anxious to adopt protective coloring, to become like one of the natives, to discard the trappings of Western elitism as soon as possible upon arrival in the village, to bring out the tape recorder and video camera only after having observed all the rituals of introduction; because otherwise the natives might show embarrassing submission, troublesome resistance, or sullen resentment at being the objects of scientific scrutiny.

It is no surprise that Bloom also deplores historicism: he would probably observe that we are attracted to early music because it is a distraction from our own creative exhaustion.

Planners of curricula are struggling to combine a mandate from the sixties with a mandate from the eighties and nineties: "diversity requirements" as part of "core requirements." In place of the former "multiversity" and the "cafeteria of courses," there must now be a core of liberal arts and science that is the common inheritance of every student—yet this same core must somehow open new windows on the diversity of the world. At the University of Maryland, for instance, the new undergraduate curriculum requires "one course that focuses primarily on either (a) the history, status, treatment, or accomplishments of women or minority groups and subcultures, or (b) cultural areas outside North America and Western Europe."[29]

At the moment the scholars who are eager to throw open the new windows seem to be outnumbering, or at least out-talking, those who want to stay warm inside the old library of "great books of the Western world." At the 1989 meeting of the Modern Language Association in Washington, D.C., some six hundred of the approximately three thousand papers delivered were primarily concerned with ideas about gender and sexual preference in literature.[30] And the 1990 joint meeting of the Society for Ethnomusicology, the Society for Music Theory, and the American Musicological Society at Oakland, California broke new ground in its papers, performances, demonstrations, panel discussions, and addresses on feminism and gender studies, sexual preference, folk music, rock, jazz, pop, Afro-American music, semiotics, new approaches to criticism, and alternate value systems—with less attention than ever before to the idea of a "canon." (Yet since then the tide seems to have receded somewhat; see the conclusion of this study.)

Anthropology vs. passion

All this reminds us that ethnomusicology, being partly the offspring of anthropology, increasingly emphasizes the topic of mankind around the world as the starting point of any description of musics. If man is the proper study of mankind, it follows that the anthropological vantage point must be above reproach, and that where the tradition of history and of musical composition is oral rather than written, such a vantage point seems especially appropriate. For instance, in studying music as an aspect of social behavior it may be beside the point to pursue the quintessentially Western task of notating music traditionally transmitted by oral-aural means, such as the recitation of Yugoslav epics or the improvisations of Charlie Parker. More rewarding in the anthropological view might be the astonishing panorama of epic recitation from Homer to the present, or an understanding of the drug culture in jazz. This approach may succeed in avoiding many of the questions that some

[29]*Promises to Keep: The College Park Plan for Undergraduate Education*, a report prepared by the Ad Hoc Committee on Undergraduate Education of the College Park Campus Senate, 1987, p. 31.

[30]*The Washington Post*, Dec. 29, 1989.

musicians cannot get out of their heads, such as the relation between melody type and the ten-syllable line in Yugoslav epic songs, or the chord extensions in Parker's improvisations. It does seem to many musicians, though, that "music in the life of man" becomes a bleak proposition unless it includes the details of individual works of art in a comparative and even an evaluative, or critical, fashion. Students turn to music because of their passion for music, not because they want to study sociology and anthropology and fight injustice. Passion may not be all that music has to offer; but may we all be spared the kind of student in whose emotional life music plays only a trivial part. Whatever keeps a dissertation-writer going through years of lonely labor had better include some passion if the project is going to be completed. The passion for music and the passion for knowledge are not the same, and it is a colossal mistake to assume that they are.

It is also a mistake, of course, to suppose that one can be most gratified by art without a heavy investment of labor that may itself lack artistic passion. Keats wrote an immortal poem "On First Looking into Chapman's Homer," but it was Chapman, not Keats—the positivist, not the critic—who through a great effort of restoration finally achieved the more gratifying understanding of Homer.

Ethnomusicology deals more profitably with the outward, salient, sociological circumstances of music than does historical musicology, partly because in orally transmitted music such circumstances constitute a greater part of the art work, and partly because notated music alone can communicate meaningfully even when it is excised from its cultural context.

East is East and West is also East

Be all that as it may, it has been for centuries part of the very fiber of Western culture to study and absorb the rest of the planet's cultures, whether in the spirit of greed, political advantage, benevolence, arrogance, curiosity, or scholarly detachment. The greatness and distinctiveness of Western civilization has stemmed since the Renaissance not from insular perpetuation of local beliefs and customs, not from fearful submission to authority, not from tribal preservation of ancestral error, but from the revived spirit of the Argonauts, the eagerness to sail away from familiar shores across unknown seas in search of the unknown. The sense of awe that is likely to envelop an informed observer of a great city of the West—London, for example— comes not merely from an awareness of all that has been felt, said, and done down the centuries within those very precincts, but also from the knowledge that many threads in that rich tapestry of art, science, and life came from far-away places. If the British Museum might be considered a microcosm of everything that defines Western society, then our informed observer must be duly impressed by the attention devoted there to artifacts from *outside* Britain, from Grecian temples to Chinese vases, from Egyptian sarcophagi to Tibetan scroll paintings. In other words, without its knowledge and even its exploitation of the non-West, the genius of Western society would be profoundly poorer.

Back to the paradox of ethnocentrism vs. cultural relativism, then: the ethnomusicologist very properly wants to avoid that greatest of all ethnomusicological evils, the arrogant assignment of comparative *values* to different musics—but his very "discovery" of non-Western musics in the first place has to depend upon his godlike ability to approach them from above, to pick them up and set them down in comparative arrays, like museum artifacts much admired but still sorted, organized, described, exhibited (how can one avoid saying "evaluated"?) as mere artifacts by an all-seeing, all-encompassing (how can one avoid saying "superior"?) intelligence.

Questioning the canon

One of the most unsettling results of the ethnomusicological campaign against ethnocentrism is a reassessment of the value of Western classical music. In this reassessment, which is now the daily bread of many faculties of musicology, the canon of Western masterpieces, and the ceaseless labors of historical musicologists in restoring the Western music of the past, might be seen as another aspect of European elitism, imperialism, even musical apartheid. Why not open your eyes, asks the ethnomusicologist, and discover for yourselves and your students that, for instance, harmony and polyphony are not the exclusive invention of the West? Why not indeed? And while we're at it, how about more explorations of the relations between present-day improvised and early written polyphony, between modern forms of improvised recitation and theories of narration and certain notated forms of chant, between the written cosmogonies of medieval music theorists and the orally transmitted cosmogonies of non-literate cultures, between Western and non-Western teleological ideas of musical form. . . . But who is asking such questions on university campuses in North America? Primarily those immersed in Western ways of thinking, which have to include the canon of Western art music. Furthermore, as noted above, it is a single consciousness that seeks to know the remote object of art, whether that object is remote in place or in time; ethnomusicologists and historical musicologists are twins. They cannot logically find fault with each others' interests.

Far-from-identical twins

Twins or not, there has not yet been any true integration of musicology with ethnomusicology, neither in the all-encompassing sense that Charles Seeger envisioned nor in any more specialized sense. Not very long ago it seemed to be an article of faith that such integration would inevitably take place. Claude Palisca, mentioned above as a perceptive commentator on musicological trends, predicted in 1970[31] that, along with new theories of musical structure, fresh computer applications in musical scholarship, and enhanced communication between musicology and music education, there would be significant growth in the ethnomusicology of Western music. There was plenty of agreement on all sides, as a glance at annual programs of the American Musicological Society around that time will show. But a decade later, in the editor's introduction to *Musicology in the 1980s: Methods, Goals, Opportunities*,[32] Palisca confessed that in the 1970 prediction he had "utterly failed at divination," because none of the predicted developments is dealt with in *Musicology in the 1980s*, which is the record of a panel discussion on musicological trends at the 1981 meeting of the American Musicological Society. In *Contemplating Music*, Joseph Kerman comments on Palisca's report with these trenchant words, already much challenged:

> If ethnomusicological methods [in musicology] have not taken, then, it is not for lack of trying. The reason for the relative failure seems clear enough to me. There are really only a limited number of areas — such as oral transmission and concepts of mode — where ethnomusicological research itself can impinge directly on the study of Western music. Western music is just too different from other musics, and its cultural contexts too

[31]In *Main Trends of Research in the Social and Human Sciences*, op. cit.
[32]Op. cit.

different from other cultural contexts. The traditional alliance of musicology has been with the humanistic disciplines, such as history, criticism, and philology, not with the social sciences. . . . It is one thing . . . to draw on modern historiography, with its ample provision for insights from anthropology and sociology, and quite another to draw on those disciplines directly for the understanding of Western music. The latter process has not had uniformly brilliant results in reference to non-Western musics, as the lingering polarization within the field of ethnomusicology testifies. Musicologists need to maintain a sharply skeptical attitude, I think, to the message they are receiving about the virtues of trying to adopt ethnomusicological methods to their own work.[33]

Kerman's whole promotion of criticism in musicology—criticism as an assessment of value—constitutes another obstacle to the employment of ethnomusicological method in historical musicology: the uniqueness and the preciousness of the individual work of art acts against any generalized socio-cultural homogenization of its meaning. It is of course not to the credit of historical musicology that its perception of music is still all too independent of social context, yet Palisca's and Kerman's assessments remain essentially valid despite several recent accounts of ethnology or sociology as an approach to historical musicology.[34]

Identical twins

Apparently nobody has yet listed in one place the well-known developments in the past century that seem to account for both Palisca's and Kerman's observations. These developments are the following: 1) For all their lip service to systematic musicology, the musical scholars of Chrysander's and Adler's time were primarily concerned with establishing definitive written records of the music of the past rather than ideas about improvisation and oral transmission, and succeeding generations of musicologists have followed in their footsteps. 2) Systematic musicology (along with anthropology), not historical musicology, has always been the natural partner of ethnomusicology. Yet historical, positivistic musicology has become much more important than systematic musicology in the eyes of the world, largely because

[33]pp. 174-5.
[34]Such as the session on "Historical Studies in Ethnomusicology" at the 1990 SEM meeting in Oakland, California.

people prefer heard music to talk about music. This natural preference has been fostered by the wholesale and largely unforeseen restoration of heard music from the past by the ironic collaboration of two institutions that had always fastidiously avoided each others' company: positivistic musicology and the mass media. 3) Western musicians and listeners, exactly like musicians and listeners around the world, have, in general, made an emotional investment in their own heard music, and therefore find it difficult to describe *that* music with ethnomusicological objectivity. They attend chamber-music recitals and operas and rock concerts not to preserve social status (as some sociologists would have it) but to experience the transcendent. They listen to recordings of Western music restored by musicologists not because they may be aware that musicologists exist but because most of that music is part of their flesh and bone. They will do a poor job of objectively describing the anthropology or the sociology of any music they have heard all their lives, whether that music is a symphony or a nineteenth-century evangelical hymn or a pop tune. By and large, they are molded and prejudiced as much by their own music as by their own education, religion, and social customs. *Their* "tribal" urge may very well come from the music of the so-called "vanishing European elite," a music which is not vanishing but becoming ubiquitous, sometimes pushing other traditions aside and sometimes integrating with those traditions, around the globe— even though is has to compete with a swelling stream of vulgarity. The ubiquity of that music does not make it any less tribal or any more susceptible to ethnomusicological description by scholars who were born and raised in the middle of it. It is that paradox again: only insiders can really know it, but—if we seek an objective description of it—only outsiders can describe it to other outsiders. If there is a defense of deconstruction as applied to music, I suggest this one. 4) Systematic musicology springs from the compulsion to talk about music, to find humane meaning in music through various forms of investigation not necessarily involving the hearing and study of individual compositions. That compulsion has dignified the calling of musician since antiquity. It will not be denied, no matter how broad and deep the flood of heard music at every level, from the sublime to the Muzaked. This means that systematic musicology will always be with us despite being overshadowed by historical musicology. "Far from being a kind of 'dumping ground' for matters of secondary interest to historians," wrote Vincent Duckles in the splendid *New Grove* article on musicology, "the systematic approach has come to be regarded as leading to fundamental research into the nature and properties of music, not only as an art but as a sociological, acoustical and psychological phenomenon."[35]

Here, then, is where musicology and ethnomusicology have the best chance of integration. Whereas it might always be difficult or awkward to apply ethnomusicology to historical musicology, ethnomusicology and systematic musicology have been together from the beginning. The grand questions about the role of music in society, in human consciousness, in the cosmos, have always occupied literate and non-literate thinkers alike. For instance, what scholar of whatever persuasion would not be fascinated by the association between timbre and musical style? The systematic-ethnomusicological approach to this question might cause a breakthrough in historical musicology's approach to it. An "ancient Chinese musical dictionary . . . contained six terms for the sound of struck stone, six for jade, six for wood. . . ."[36] One loud "Hey baby" from a passing boom box eloquently identifies a style. On hearing only the first note of *The Rite of Spring*—just that one high note chirped by the bassoon, after which I stopped the record—half the graduate students in my seminar correctly identified the work. Whatever all the instantaneously perceptible factors of style may be, surely timbre, or what Jan LaRue calls "sound" to include other instantaneously perceptible factors, is the deadest giveaway. Yet in all the formal, harmonic, and contrapuntal analysis around us, we say very little about this basic aspect of music. Ethnomusicology can properly fill this gap by imposing a worldwide perspective on the vast network of meaning communicated by timbre, "sound," "tone of voice." Only ethnomusicology can show singers of opera and lieder that the "legitimate" voice is just one of many considered legitimate outside their narrowly defined, if highly valued, circle: jazz, pop, rock, folk, plus the whole checkerboard of non-Western vocal timbres and what they might teach us about Western vocal timbres in the Middle Ages and the Renaissance. (The wondrous technological apparatus that made modern ethnomusicology possible at the beginning of this century, and that now makes musically meaningful—even quantifiable—comparisons of timbre possible, is the same technology that has flooded the world with the heard music produced by historical musicology.)

---

[35]Op. cit.

[36]Mantle Hood in *Musicology*, op. cit., p. 258, citing a scholarly paper by Laurence Picken.

Siblings

This is not to devalue the rich liaisons that will occasionally be possible between *historical* musicology and ethnomusicology without any mediation. Radio stations specializing in broadcasting classical music, as institutions fed by the work of historical musicologists, provide a good example: most of them drag their feet maddeningly when asked to be more adventurous in their programming. That is why no historical musicologist worthy of the name would hesitate to dump certain bits and pieces of the commonly broadcast canon of Western art music—say, Mozart's execrable German Dances or Beethoven's detestable Variations on "See the Conqu'ring Hero Comes" from Handel's *Judas Maccabeus*—in order to hear instead a passionate Indian raga, a fine shakuhachi performance, an intricate gamelan piece. (I hope nobody will offer here, of all places, the Mickey-Mouse comment that we should not impose upon others our own judgment as to what is good and what is bad.) Ethnomusicology shakes up historical musicology in wonderful ways. One last example: Oral tradition is valid. The quest for authenticity in the restoration of early notated music is valid. Therefore all the inflated and doctored versions of *Messiah* from the eighteenth century to the present are valid. Therefore the most strenuous attempts to discover and perform *Messiah* in the versions known to Handel are valid.

As the definition of "classical music" continues to change in the West through new perceptions of the canon of Western music and its cultural contexts, there will also be new understandings of music outside the Western classical tradition, and various forms of integration will take place in vast areas of the world, such as the Pacific Rim. It would be nothing less than suicidal for ethnomusicology, a product of the West, not to treasure its own inheritance of classical music, the indispensable background against which is silhouetted not only its own understanding of the non-Western, its own judgment as to what *is* supposedly non-Western, but the very shape of its own soul and body, the expression on its face, the light in its eyes. No historical musicologist of any stripe feels like integrating with an ethnomusicologist who stands outside the library of Western music and chants, "Burn, baby, burn." But I hasten to add that my own primary motivation some years ago in working to establish the ethnomusicology program at the University of Maryland was to put music not belonging to the Western art tradition into the ears of student *composers* of Western music, even more than the ears of student *musicologists*, in the hope of cross-fertilization. The heart of our musical life is kept beating by composers, not musicologists, not theorists, not performers, not teachers. In the hermetic atmosphere of many a festival of contemporary music, I often recall, with hope, what Helen Roberts said more than fifty years ago:

> Like everything else in life, left to grow alone a musical art tends to become introverted, stagnant or set in special ways—ways so strangely limited among certain groups, despite the great possibilities for growth and development inherent in the musical material itself. For new development there must seemingly be a fusion of different heritages. Musicians need to know with more complete understanding and sympathy, how alien musics are made, and to appreciate their beauties which to many, alas, are so obscure. Only when some non-European forms are as clearly understood and as keenly enjoyed as our own will composers feel their way into new and greater music of the future, built up from their combined beauties.[37]

Since the whole world seems to be ethnomusicological, curriculum-planning in ethnomusicology has to be a process of selection rather than collection. The ethnomusicology curriculum must give our graduate students the ability to chart a good course on an endless ocean.

---

[37]In the *Proceedings* of the Music Teachers National Association, 1936, quoted by Mantle Hood in *Musicology*, op. cit., p. 305.

FOREGROUND

Prerequisites to Consideration for Admission to the Graduate School and to Graduate Studies in Musicology

A comment on prerequisites and performing ability

There is little disagreement that the best raw material for a graduate program in musicology is an educated musician, a liberal artist well versed in musicianship. But, by the testimony of many a graduate advisor, the term "educated musician" is nearly an oxymoron among the great majority of graduating seniors in music. In a curriculum survey of 1935,[1] Randall Thompson described the impossibility of offering professional musical training as part of any bachelor's degree worthy of the name. He believed that colleges and universities should produce enlightened, well-rounded amateurs of music and leave the creation of professional musicians to the conservatories. A large part of this attitude was imported from British universities, which in the 1930s offered only a few Mus.B. degrees, primarily to prospective music teachers and church organists, while upholding for the bulk of its musically inclined undergraduates the old Elizabethan ideal of the gentleman amateur. (The Doctor of Music in Britain has traditionally been given only to established composers, and the Ph.D. for research in music was extremely rare there until well after World War II. The professional training of British musicians has almost always been assigned to the conservatories.)

By 1957 Manfred Bukofzer, the eminent German expatriate who had been at BERKELEY since 1941, noted sadly[2] that most American universities were rushing away from Randall Thompson's prescription as fast as possible, that the impossible combination of professional training *in* music and education *for* music was being universally institutionalized in the undergraduate university curriculum. He attributed this development to a misunderstanding of the admirable and unique American ambition to educate everybody: although the original goal was to spread music appreciation, to produce a happy race of musical amateurs, musical professionalism—musical vocationalism—unfortunately proved to be an inseparable part of the package, imported from and competing with the conservatory. The result has typically been an

---

[1] *College Music: An Investigation for the Association of American Colleges* (New York).
[2] In *The Place of Musicology in American Institutions of Higher Learning* (New York).

undergraduate curriculum in music that attempts to produce professional performers and composers on the one hand and broadly educated scholars on the other hand, while not accomplishing either goal very well.

The German system that had produced Bukofzer cleanly separated the functions of university and conservatory. It was easy for him to visualize a graduating senior who performed and composed well enough to gain a musicianly understanding, but who could also think critically and write clearly, who had really studied music history and theory along with languages, history, philosophy, science, literature. Yet surely Bukofzer would have agreed that the German system was not without serious faults. If he had lived a few more years he would have listened seriously to his countryman Friedrich Blume, who said in 1968:

> The beginner in the study of historical musicology should make his start with two fields of fundamental learning: with music and with languages. When I say "With music," this seems to be a truism. But it is not. In my long career as a professor of musicology I have learned that a good many students lack this basis. They confuse "reading musicology" with "learning music." The consequence is that they find themselves unexpectedly involved in the questions of medieval modes before having a command of harmony, or entangled in the niceties of the *chiavette* before ever having learned how to read normal clefs. First of all it is, in my view, absolutely essential that a beginner in musicology have a fairly ample knowledge of the music existing in a certain field and that he be able to sing or play this music. It is not too important whether the chosen field is the music of the Netherlanders of the fifteenth century or the music of German Romanticism or Italian Baroque. For obvious reasons, it is desirable and useful to know the literature of music from Haydn to Brahms in any case. But whatever field he may choose, it is indispensable that the beginning student of musicology have a thorough knowledge of the music in his chosen field. It is of paramount importance for him to have a firm basis in one field, because this assures a standard by which to measure all other music he may come to know in the course of his studies. The one sort of music he knows and loves and of which he has a well-founded concept will serve him as a key to others. I have often observed that students who lack this firm basis and who have no inner connection with any sort of music at all never achieve an understanding for the more uncommon and more distant kinds of music. Time and again I have told my own students that anyone who lacks this firm basis is likely to be one of those wretched musicologists who can describe in detail the construction of a Machaut motet or analyze the serial structure of a twelve-tone piece, but have never experienced the meaning of any music.

Coordinating the study of practical music with graduate musicology should be easier in America than in Germany, because in the United States the training in practical music and the study of musicology are often to be found at the same university and under one roof. In Germany, practical music is studied at conservatories and professional schools, which have nothing to do with the university, while musicology is studied at the university. Thus one area of study tends to exclude the other, although the division is not as sharp as it was twenty or thirty years ago. In the universities of the United States it seems to me that it should be quite possible for the performer to train himself in both aspects of his art. You may envy us our practical musicians who study musicology; we envy you the many excellent practical musicians you have at your universities.[3]

Should a musicology student continue to study performance after he or she has begun graduate work? Or should a budding musicologist follow the Aristotelian pattern[4] of studying performance only up to a point—that point being merely to gain understanding? As can be seen below, one might impute the Aristotelian attitude to such institutions as COLUMBIA, among other Ivy-League universities still variously attached to their European predecessors and situated in the midst of a rich urban array of professional performances. But, for three main reasons, it has become very common on less urban campuses to demand continued involvement in performance from students doing graduate work in musicology: for their own greater musical understanding, for their contribution to the university's concert life, and to enhance their prospects of gainful employment after graduation. In the musically rich city as in the musically deprived boondocks there is no substitute for being surrounded by and helping to produce live music, especially if it is all a matter of love; at that level we find it quite impossible to agree with Aristotle that professional performance is a "vulgar pleasure."

---

[3]Part of the Inaugural Lectures of the Ph.D. Program in Music at the City University of New York, published as *Perspectives in Musicology*, ed. by Barry S. Brook, Edward O.D. Downes, and Sherman van Solkema (New York, 1972), pp. 17-18, 29.

[4]See the quotation from Aristotle's *Politics*, trans. by H. Rackham, in *Source Readings in Music History*, selected and annotated by Oliver Strunk (New York, 1950), pp. 13-24 and especially 19-21, "since we reject professional education in the instruments and in performance ...." Aristotle and medieval scholars after him considered musical performance to be a mere physical skill, like juggling. Although that idea is still alive in many liberal-arts institutions, it is hardly ever mentioned today, when performance can be considered to be a special form of musicological positivism and even one of the higher forms of criticism.

Thus IOWA, to take one extreme example, lists "a high level" of performance ability as a prerequisite to admission in musicology before it gets around to mentioning a liberal-arts background. INDIANA even requires an audition and, if needed, "remedial" instruction in performance. Such schools have no large metropolitan area nearby to give them the best live music; they must do it all themselves, at all levels and in all performance media. They are the new Maecenases of music, successors to the church, the aristocracy, the box office, and the state in the history of musical patronage. They have to be, in order to satisfy the high population of university intellectuals who demand the best music even in rural surroundings. As for the music faculty in such a place, the alternative is impossible: to teach music where good live music is seldom heard. Viewed from this standpoint, the production of Wagner operas by a university nestled among Indiana cornfields does not seem so strange. Perhaps even Bukofzer might see the reason behind such a phenomenon. Gustave Reese saw the reason, even though he spoke from the calm security of NYU, whose musicology students, among the best in the nation, apparently have little need to prove themselves as finished performers:

> . . . it is a plain fact that many conservatories are losing their independence; universities are providing havens for so-called "Schools of Music" — that is, for conservatories. Thus, we increasingly find on the American scene a situation in which a body of musicologically oriented faculty and students and a body of faculty and students dedicated to performance are thrown together under the same roof. Peaceful co-existence between these schools and the more musicologically oriented departments may not always be easy to achieve. But the fact is that the practical and the scholarly branches of music are going to be thrown together more and more, and some form of cooperation between them must be achieved. And, if safeguards are adopted, there is no reason why this cooperation should not be workable, and even beneficial.

* * *

We need more bridges between the practical and scholarly sides of music. These bridges are being built on the American university scene. To quote Denis Stevens: "To most European observers, such an arrangement is hair-raising and heretical. Yet when they observe from a closer vantage point and for a reasonable period of time, they generally admit that the system works much better than seemed possible."[5]

Only in America, and probably only in the rural Midwest, could philosophical questions about musical performance vs. musical scholarship be brought to a circumstance unprecedented in two and a half millennia. At INDIANA, the age-old questions about performing as a way of knowing are answered by the quintessentially American expedient of putting scholars and performers together in seemingly every possible juxtaposition. The picture is neatly drawn in the university's printed announcement of its hundreds of graduate and undergraduate music courses. Even the method of identifying music courses at Indiana shows a hard-won administrative control over every aspect of study in this unique musical community. The accumulated musical creations of Western civilization are reduced to a single master list of specialties, alphabetically arranged.

If among musicologists in general there is an Aristotelian antipathy against performers, that feeling is well disguised. On the contrary—at national meetings of the American Musicological Society or the Society for Ethnomusicology, for instance—performers seem to be more frequently embraced than disdained. Every other musicologist one meets in the hotel lobby is still active as a performer; and in these days of the early-music revival, the non-Western concert, and the devotion to repertories outside the classical mainstream it would be not only foolish and false but also suicidal to pronounce, as one of my European-ized teachers did long ago, that "performers are the bootblacks of music."

But back we come to the plight of the new graduate student in musicology. Because she has devoted so much of her life to the practice room, she knows little about the foreign languages in which the history of her chosen discipline resides; she has only the shakiest grasp of history itself, not to mention literature and philosophy; quite often she has been granted a baccalaureate degree without having to write a real research paper or a real essay test. If she must provide musical performances more for the commonweal than for her own profit, when she might be remedying her academic deficiencies herself, she is being placed at a

---

[5]Reese's opening Inaugural Lecture of the Ph.D. program at CUNY in 1968, published in *Perspectives in Musicology*, op.cit., pp. 11-12. The Stevens quotation is from Stevens's review of *Musicology*, op.cit., in *The Musical Times*, CV (Feb. 1964), p. 112.

disadvantage, at least in the immediate sense. Perhaps in the long run, like a great number of musicologists today, she will be enriched by all that performing; perhaps not. It takes all kinds to make music. If she goes to a strong performance school she will be a certain kind of musicologist. If she does her graduate work on a campus where student performance is incidental or irrelevant, she will become another kind. *De gustibus non disputandum.*

In either case, it makes no sense to conclude that the highly desirable association of performers and scholars *must* be underlined by placing them under the same *administrative* umbrella. Particularly in an urban setting, the needs of the musical scholars on the university faculty are likely to be so different from the needs of the performers on the same faculty that the two groups should be administratively and fiscally independent even as they work intimately together.

Prerequisites on paper

ALL: A baccalaureate from a recognized institution, transcripts, recommendations, statement of purpose or essay.

MOST: Graduate Record Examination. MOST: The music section of the GRE is not required. That may change now that the music section of the GRE has been revised.

MOST: Undergraduate grade point average of at least 3.0. UNT: Undergraduate GPA of at least 3.0 on the last 60 hours or 2.8 on all undergraduate work; a student with an undergraduate GPA below that may be admitted provisionally and may be required to take special examinations. INDIANA: "A student who does not have an undergraduate and graduate grade average of 3.0 or better may be admitted on probation in exceptional cases. The probationary status continues until the entering proficiency exams and 15 hours of course work have been satisfactorily completed."

MOST: Ranking high enough competitively. It is obvious that a student whose undergraduate GPA is only 3.0 or not much higher is at a disadvantage in being considered for admission to the musicology program, even though such a GPA may satisfy the graduate school. Between the lines is the message that a great many subjective factors may work either against or in favor of the student's chance of admission.

MOST: Samples of previous work.

NYU, CUNY GRADUATE CENTER: Superior academic record, as shown by transcripts, recommendations, GRE scores. Strong background in liberal arts and a special emphasis on music. NC: The baccalaureate should be comparable to NC's baccalaureate. PRINCETON: "Entering students are expected to have had substantially the same preparation in the history and theory of music as that required for the A.B. degree at Princeton." ILLINOIS: The bachelor's degree or its equivalent should be "comparable in content and in number of credit hours with that granted by the University of Illinois at Urbana-Champaign." HARVARD: Distinguished undergraduate background. YALE: Musical talent, strong background in liberal arts and foreign languages, good writing ability, and a scholarly bent.

COLUMBIA, NYU: A solid grounding in the history and theory of Western music. COLUMBIA: Undergraduate work must have included not less than 3 years (90 points) of liberal arts courses. Excluded is work in such fields as applied music, architecture, business, dramatic arts, education, law, military science, painting, sculpture, speech, and writing. ILLINOIS: A prerequisite for admission to the Ph.D. program is "a minimum of 32 semester hours in the liberal arts and sciences, normally including general history, philosophy, and literature." MICHIGAN: 12 semester hours of music history, 12 of theory, and "a liberal arts sequence in addition to the foreign language and English requirements." UNT: At least 24 semester hours of undergraduate work in music, 12 of which must be advanced. USC: "Applicants should have an undergraduate degree with a major in music; . . . 18 units or equivalent in theory, including harmony, analytical techniques, and counterpoint; 8 units or equivalent in music history and literature; and at least 16 units in history, literature, or the arts other than music." WASHINGTON: "The undergraduate program should have included . . . reasonably comprehensive" liberal-arts studies, including history, English literature, fine arts, and languages; 4 years of music history; 3 years of theory.

BERKELEY, PENN, CUNY GRADUATE CENTER: Departmental examination proctored by a professor of music at the applicant's current university or college, and mailed in as part of the application: sight-singing, melodic and harmonic dictation, harmony and counterpoint, history of music. BERKELEY and CUNY provide sample examinations on request.

COLUMBIA, YALE, HARVARD: Interview, if possible. YALE, PENN: Attend some classes and meet with faculty, if possible. ALL: Visits to the campus and chats with faculty are obviously encouraged, even if not specifically mentioned in announcements.

COLUMBIA: Ability to play the piano, read orchestral scores. USC: Performance ability "in at least one field of applied music, including piano." WASHINGTON: Professional performance training, sufficient preparation in piano, and some performance in ensembles. IOWA: "Students are expected to have some proficiency at the keyboard and a high level of ability in some performance area." (Only in the next sentence does Iowa's announcement say that "a reasonable background in other fine arts, history and literature is also required.") MICHIGAN: "Students should have attained proficiency in some field of performance. From a practical standpoint, college positions frequently require the ability to combine teaching in music history with instruction in the field of performance. From a musical standpoint, nothing can replace the first-hand experience of actively performing music." WEST VIRGINIA: The applicant must "demonstrate performance ability on the major instrument or voice [at a level determined by the faculty]. When the performance medium is not a keyboard instrument, performance [at a lower level] on piano is also required. Students who have not yet attained these levels at entrance but are not significantly below them may take private lessons as electives in order to meet them, provided they are met by the end of the second year." UBC (a cautionary note about ethnomusicology): "An applicant in ethnomusicology who holds a Bachelor's degree in a field other than music is expected to have a strong academic background in music and should have studied a musical instrument for some years."

INDIANA: All musicology students "are required to demonstrate in person to a faculty auditioning committee a minimum level of performance ability equivalent to the end of the fourth year for concentrations in that area. . . . Failure to meet the required level will automatically indicate probationary admission and will require additional performance study in each period of enrollment as a prerequisite to the desired degree. A tape may be used for preliminary acceptance into the School of Music; however, a personal audition is required of all music majors for official acceptance into graduate degree programs."

A comment on foreign-language background

Despite warnings that knowledge of foreign languages is a *prerequisite* for success in musicology graduate programs, and even though some institutions list foreign-language ability among their requirements for *admission* even at the master's level, the topic continues to be mentioned by all, as noted in various places below, in lists of *post-admission* requirements for degrees, along with strategies for meeting the language requirement, deadlines, and so forth. The obvious message is that foreign-language proficiency already attained makes the student a more desirable candidate for admission, but that many or most students will have to continue foreign language study after admission. And, of course, it is a standard event in the lives of many American graduate students that, after surviving for awhile in regular course work, they crash spectacularly and disappear permanently after the last deadline for language tests has come and gone. They are products of the continued indifference to foreign languages in the U.S., where translators are thought of as a kind of audiovisual equipment. A second standard event is the channeling of a lifetime of scholarship into categories determined not by what the student really likes or what musicology really needs, but by the student's choice of foreign languages to study. We like to say, for instance, that the real history of Spanish music has not yet been written; we don't say that we neglect Spanish music largely because Spanish brings up the rear in the customary list of required foreign languages.

COLUMBIA: For historical musicology, a reading knowledge of German and of French or Latin; for ethnomusicology, German and French; provision for removal of deficiencies. USC: Applicants for admission "should have . . . competency in French or German. . . ." MICHIGAN: The applicant "should be prepared in German, French, or another foreign language." NC: In the list of prerequisites for admission is this statement: "M.A. candidates must pass the departmental examination in one modern foreign language; Ph.D. candidates, in two." KANSAS: "The applicant is expected to have a reading knowledge of German or French. A language deficiency may be satisfied after entrance into the program." ILLINOIS: "Applicants in musicology must give evidence of a reading knowledge of French or German. Students otherwise admissible may satisfy any language deficiencies concurrently with graduate studies."

Institutional Policies on Admission

BERKELEY: Graduate students are admitted in the Fall semester only. Those holding only the baccalaureate are admitted to the M.A. program only, not directly to the Ph.D. program. On obtaining the M.A. the student is advised whether he or she may continue to the Ph.D. Those already possessing the M.A. or its equivalent will be considered for admission to the Ph.D. curriculum if they submit appropriate samples of their work. PENN: "The department discourages admission in the Spring semester, but it is willing to consider it under very special circumstances. Generally, financial assistance is not available for students entering the program in the Spring semester."

HARVARD: Admission is only for the Ph.D. "There is no admission to an A.M. program separate from the Ph.D. program. In unusual cases, students who cannot successfully complete the General Examination [see page 86] may be given the option of completing the requirements for a terminal A.M. degree."

CUNY GRADUATE CENTER: Admission is only for the Ph.D. An "en route" M.A. is awarded at 45 credits after the first examination (see page 83) is passed at 30 credits.

ILLINOIS, KANSAS, UT AT AUSTIN, COLORADO, TORONTO, UBC, SUNY STONY BROOK, INDIANA: A master's degree or its equivalent is among the requirements for admission to the Ph.D. program.

MICHIGAN: Admission to the Ph.D. program in historical musicology requires a master's degree in music history or musicology and a knowledge of at least 2 major foreign languages, one of which must be German. Admission to the Ph.D. program in ethnomusicology requires a master's *thesis* in ethnomusicology; the thesis may be written elsewhere and submitted for approval, or the student may be conditionally admitted until the master's thesis requirement is fulfilled at Michigan. (Language requirements for the ethnomusicology Ph.D. may be met after admission, if necessary.) The ethnomusicology student transferring with a master's degree from another institution must take a diagnostic examination in music *theory*.

YALE: Of 40–70 applications received each year for graduate study in musicology, only about 15–16 are admitted. In the past decade the department of music at Yale has awarded about 4–6 Ph.Ds annually. HARVARD: In the entire university, only about a tenth of the applicants for graduate study eventually enroll. NYU: The musicology programs "are deliberately small, admitting only a few students each year." PENN: The total number of graduate students in all programs of the music department is no more than 40–50 in a given year.

MARYLAND, UT AT AUSTIN, KANSAS, ILLINOIS, WISCONSIN, UNT: These are the only institutions among the ones surveyed that offer the M.M. in musicology rather than the M.A. INDIANA offers both. Except at Indiana, there seems to be little consistent difference between M.M. and M.A. curricula. At Indiana the M.M. requires slightly more performance and slightly less academic course work than the M.A.

Requirements for the Master's Degree in Musicology

ALL: Non-credit remedial study required, either as determined by tests or in a form standardized for all students. See page 49.

ALL: The curriculum must be chosen with the guidance of one or more faculty advisors.

MOST: Minimum GPA of 3.0 for all graduate work. Some require a higher GPA; none will accept a lower.

MOST: A residence requirement of at least 2 semesters, three quarters, or one academic year, variously defined, and with adjustments for part-time.

Maximum credit toward the Master's for suitable courses taken elsewhere

("Suitable" in that they are appropriate substitutions, were awarded a grade of "B" or better, were not part of an already-earned degree, and were completed not too long ago)

MICHIGAN, UNT: 6 semester hours. COLUMBIA: One course. BERKELEY: "Certain of the course requirements . . . may be waived by the Graduate Committee on the basis of equivalent course work already completed with distinction." PENN: "No work done at other institutions may be counted toward the requirements for the A.M. degree." INDIANA: None. MARYLAND: 6 semester hours. ILLINOIS: A petition for transfer of credit may be submitted after the successful completion of at least 2 units of graduate work at Urbana-Champaign. (One unit = approximately 4 semester hours.)

OTHERS, where transfer credit is not mentioned: The concise specificity of some lists of course requirements (e.g., YALE's "8 courses") apparently means that no transfer credit is given; the option-filled panorama of courses in other curricula (e.g., at NC) apparently means that a modest amount of transfer credit might be given.

Full time vs. part time

MICHIGAN, HARVARD, COLUMBIA, PENN: All graduate students are expected to work full-time on their degrees. MOST: This is also clearly implied in many other program descriptions, as where requirements are spelled out as belonging to the "first year," "second year," etc. One cannot assume, however, that only the less renowned programs offer the option of part-time attendance. At NYU, for instance, full-time is 12 points per semester and part-time is no fewer than 8 points per semester; a typical graduate course counts 4 points. In general, there is a more liberal attitude toward part-time work for the master's degree than for the Ph.D.; for example, at YALE the M.A. may be pursued part-time, but not the Ph.D. except under very unusual circumstances.

Time limits

UNT, MICHIGAN, and others by implication: The M.A. must be completed within 6 years. MARYLAND: 5 years. COLUMBIA: "A student who fails to complete all the requirements for the degree within four consecutive terms and who wishes to continue work into a fifth term must obtain the written approval of the department chairman and special permission from the Dean. If permission is granted, the student must then register continuously until all the requirements for the degree have been fulfilled." YALE: The M.A. is designed to be completed in one year of full-time work. INDIANA: 5 years, except for students whose entire degree program is taken in summer sessions, in which case 7 years.

Diagnostic examinations after admission

The existence of diagnostic examinations and non-credit remedial procedures in virtually all programs is testimony to the diversity of American postgraduates: a barely adequate student may be accepted into a barely adequate or forgivingly liberal musicology program and given a remedial course to bring his general performance up to a minimum standard; but an excellent student, accepted into an excellent or merely rigid program, may need a remedial course of the same title only because his background is spotty. In my own writing and grading of diagnostic examinations at two state universities I have found that they are most useful in testing general musicianship first and academic background second. That seems to be the case at most universities, judging from the printed descriptions. Is it also generally true that most students end up taking the same remedial courses? If so, perhaps more institutions should cut the Gordian knot as NC, HARVARD, and CHICAGO have done (see below), merely requiring every student to master the same basic musical hurdles, doing away with complex diagnostic examinations, saving considerable effort and expense in the process.

"Remedial work" is a standard rather than an exceptional aspect of most graduate musicology programs. That is not wholly owing to the inadequacy of undergraduate curricula; it is also a plain indication of the amorphous structure of the discipline. Which is not to say that musicology is ready for standardization, like medicine or accounting. On the contrary, its continued vitality is undoubtedly a result of the diversity of its aims. Diagnostic examinations are a price that must be paid to keep this diversity. The music section of the Graduate Record Examination has recently been revised;[6] that ought to be enough standardization of entrance requirements for the time being.

> . . . I know of [no] reason why we should quarrel with the man who sees the end of musicology in faithful performance, or with him who sees it in sociological interpretation, or with the one who sees it in the integration of music into the whole of a cultural epoch. And I should most agree with him who believes in the integration of as many approaches as he can

---

[6]See James Haar, Severine Neff, Janet M. Palumbo, Mari A. Pearlman, Don M. Randel, Frederick C. Tillis, Gary Wittlich, and Eugene K. Wolf, *A Description of the Revised GRE Music Test* (Princeton, 1988). The new GRE in music devotes 50 minutes to music history and 120 minutes to music theory.

master. It is exactly the multiplicity of ends and the variety of views that make for the richness and vitality of a scholarly discipline.[7]

MARYLAND: A placement examination "to assess background in music history, musical style, dictation, and analysis," plus a short test in expository writing on any musical topic. NYU: A diagnostic examination in harmony, counterpoint, orchestration, and analysis. Any deficiencies must be remedied before taking the general examination (see page 61) and before completing the second year of course work. SUNY STONY BROOK: An examination in ear training, basic keyboard skills, chorale harmonization, composition in free counterpoint in 16th- or 18th-century style, music history. Suitable undergraduate or graduate courses are required to make up for deficiencies. UBC: A placement examination in "keyboard proficiency, music history, and music theory, normally excepting the field of major study, as an aid to determination of needs in these basic areas of concern to all programs." "Students unprepared for study at the Master's level, but showing some promise for such study, may be admitted to a qualifying year to strengthen their credentials for admission. Students in a qualifying year are not admitted to the Faculty of Graduate Studies."

INDIANA: "During the week of registration and in the first few weeks of each semester, all new graduate students (M.S. students excepted), including graduates of Indiana University, are required to take a number of exams that serve as proficiency tests or prerequisites for entrance to graduate courses. Courses to remedy deficiencies indicated by these exams should be taken at the earliest opportunity. *A student is presumed deficient in any area in which the proficiency exam is not taken.*" Indiana's proficiency examinations and remedying procedures are the most elaborate among all the universities surveyed. "Students with a cumulative average of 3.0 or better are admitted conditionally until the entering proficiency exams have been passed. If the proficiency exams are not taken in advance of registration, or if the results of the examinations show deficiencies in one or more areas, the conditional status continues until the proficiency exams are passed or courses to remove deficiencies are taken. With a conditional admission, the student is registered on a semester-to- semester basis, provided that the quality of work is satisfactory for the graduate level and that a 3.0 average in all courses required for the degree is maintained."

[7]Edward E. Lowinsky, "Character and Purposes of American Musicology: A Reply to Joseph Kerman," *Journal of the American Musicological Society* 18 (Summer 1965), p. 234.

MICHIGAN: A placement examination in music *theory* is required upon admission, unless the student has had a graduate course in theory at Michigan during the past 4 years. This examination is described very elaborately in the Michigan program announcement. IOWA: An advisory examination in music history, music literature, and theory upon entrance to the program. UNT: An entrance examination in theory, history of music, music literature; a keyboard examination that consists of reading from an open score. PENN: All graduate students "must demonstrate proficiency in score reading or enroll in a non-credit remedial course." MOST: Even where there is no separate description of a diagnostic test, the existence of such a test or its equivalent should be assumed, e.g., in statements about the removal of deficiencies.

NC: As an alternative to the diagnostic examination obviously designed to eliminate waste motion, all graduate degree programs simply require a course in "Advanced Musicianship," passed with a grade of P or better: basic harmony, counterpoint, ear training, etc. HARVARD'S procedure is similar: "Music B: Exercises in Tonal Writing and Analysis is required of all graduate students and must be taken in the first year. Competence and fluency in traditional harmony, counterpoint, analysis, and strict composition are necessary prerequisites for taking the General Examination. Depending upon the student's deficiencies, more than one year of Music B may be necessary." NC and HARVARD are like NYU and MICHIGAN in emphasizing competence in theory over competence in music history and literature at the start of graduate training. At least as far as theory is concerned, a required course like those at NC and HARVARD might be a desirable alternative to the present practice at MARYLAND, in which a large number of graduate students fail the dictation part of the diagnostic examination and then partake of various classes or self-instruction schemes with various degrees of success.

CHICAGO carries the NC-HARVARD procedure a step further: "Six examinations in practical musicianship skill are administered by the Department of Music. Attainment of a satisfactory level of achievement in each skill is required for a degree. The practicum examinations are given each quarter, and are announced several weeks in advance. One or more parts may be taken at a time. Students are strongly encouraged to achieve competence at the rate of one per academic quarter, so that all have been mastered by the end of the second year of graduate study. Completion of all practicums is a Departmental requirement for the M.A. degree.

"The practicum skills tested include proficiency in sight-singing, musical dictation, and the following keyboard skills: sight-reading, figured bass, reading orchestral scores, and reading open vocal scores in 'old clefs'. The Department offers free, informal, non-credit instruction in these skills. Relevant method books are stocked each autumn in the University bookstore. A fuller description of practicum requirements, including sample examinations, is available in the Department office. . . ."

Course requirements

(Note: Some institutions list the M.A. thesis or its equivalent as a "course" and some do not. Therefore this section should be read in conjunction with the section on "Thesis or Final Document," page 63.)

The customary American distinction between master's and doctoral courses is that the former are designed mainly to convey established knowledge and the latter are intended mainly to create new knowledge. Despite that distinction, in many musicology programs M.A. and Ph.D. students sit side by side in the same seminars, and the instructor has to consult the enrollment list to tell one from the other. Indeed, it is fairly common for certain lower-level graduate courses (usually surveys of some aspect of music literature) to be open to upper-level undergraduates. One might safely assume that in such programs the faculty thinks of graduate students, especially those in the master's curriculum, as still needing to be fed knowledge in artfully and responsibly prepared doses. That kind of faculty must necessarily agree with Paul Henry Lang: "The biggest shortcoming that I find in our students today is not so much their lack of knowledge of the musicological discipline; it is the music itself that they don't know."[8] Real teachers are to be found in such faculties, along with heavy teaching loads. Senior professors might willingly teach lower-level graduate or even undergraduate courses. The university might not be as prestigious as some. Its faculty might be envious of faculties where teaching loads are low and there is more time for research.

At other universities—usually but not always the most eminent ones—every effort continues to be made to sever direct connections between the senior faculty and the undergraduate curriculum, despite a growing chorus of protest that might well cause drastic changes in, and onerous additions to, teaching loads in universities throughout the U.S. Graduate students,

[8]In *Perspectives in Musicology*, op.cit., p. 198.

especially those on the Ph.D. track, discover abruptly that they are already supposed to know music literature, among other things. They learn that to be a graduate student is to aspire to scholarly originality right away, to plunge directly into research with one's professor—who himself spends every day on the cutting edge of discovery, or at least tries daily to add something to his resumé. This is the climate that Manfred Bukofzer wanted to bring about. He deplored the widespread American conception of graduate courses as a mere continuation of undergraduate work. He wanted a wider adoption of the German ideal, according to which the primary mission of the university is to create new knowledge. As far as the most glamorous American universities were concerned, he protested too much— because from the middle of the nineteenth century to the present these universities have adopted the German model lock, stock, and barrel.

The enormous array of graduate musicology studies in American universities might be sorted out by criteria other than their emphasis or lack of emphasis on original research, of course. But it is the research factor that gives rise to the most interesting questions, pro and con. What is the value, what is the function of, say, a survey of chamber music in which the main goal is merely to soak up established knowledge about chamber music? How can humanists hold up their heads in the presence of productive scientists without advancing the frontiers of knowledge? How can American doctoral dissertations avoid the pitfalls of obscurity into which so many German dissertations have fallen, at least until recently? Why are the most famous American universities regarded as among the best in the world? What is the origin of the remarkable assumption that every graduate musicology student can be a productive researcher? How can printed announcements honestly—even proudly—offer inexperienced graduate students a chance to teach undergraduate courses without admitting that the undergraduate courses will suffer? How can a student go through four years of undergraduate courses without meeting a senior professor?

YALE: The M.A. is a one-year program designed to augment previous graduate study or as a background to further work in music history, music theory, music librarianship, performance, or composition, or to prepare for a non-academic career in journalistic criticism, curatorship, broadcasting, recording, music administration, arts administration, and so forth. The program may be undertaken full-time or part-time. It consists of 8 courses that constitute a coherent plan, particularly utilizing such Yale resources as the Musical Instrument Collection, the collection of Historical Sound Recordings, the rare book library, the Archives of Oral History-American Music, the Medieval Studies Program, the Renaissance Studies Program, and links with other departments. One course in the second semester, which may be a tutorial, leads to a major project. (This major project corresponds to the M.A. thesis.) An examination must be passed in one appropriate modern foreign language.

TORONTO: A one-year program. See page 69.

CLAREMONT: At least 30 units. Required: Introduction to research and bibliography (4 units), analysis (8), history of musical performance (4), historical courses (12), individual performance lessons or ensembles (2). Electives from ethnomusicology, Renaissance notation, organology, Bach, Handel, Verdi; "other elective alternatives are available on an irregular basis."

COLUMBIA: For historical musicology, at least 30 points of courses. The courses must include 2 semesters of proseminar in historical musicology, 2 semesters of early notation, one semester of proseminar in ethnomusicology, and 2 semesters of period seminars. For ethnomusicology, at least 30 points, which must include 2 semesters of proseminar in historical musicology, 2 semesters of proseminar in ethnomusicology, one semester of seminar in transcription and analysis, and 2 semesters of graduate anthropology courses.

WISCONSIN: In ethnomusicology, 12 credits of graduate ethnomusicology courses, 3 of thesis, 6 of bibliography and research methods, 3 of music history or theory, 6 of electives inside or outside music, total 30. At least one semester of seminar in ethnomusicology. In music history, 6 credits of bibliography and proseminar, 15 of period courses and at least two upper-level music history seminars, 9 of electives ("may include up to 4 credits of Thesis and courses in theory, ethnomusicology, and other areas"), total 30. "Majors in music history also must (1) submit to their committee a thesis or substantial seminar paper and (2) be certified competent in music theory by the theory area committee on the basis of the diagnostic examination or course work."

ILLINOIS: At least 8 units. Required: 2 units in introduction to musicology, 2 units in seminar in musicology, 2 units of thesis, and participation in an ensemble during at least 2 of the terms of study. Electives in music theory, music history, and music literature, and other courses within and outside the department of music.

INDIANA: "The total requirement for a master's degree is usually 35 hours [30 hours of academic courses plus performance] exclusive of prerequisite and deficiency courses. *Each student is required to enroll and make a passing grade in a major ensemble assigned by the dean of the School of Music each semester and summer session"* [emphasis theirs]. "Musicology at Indiana University emphasizes musical scholarship based on a foundation of sound musicianship (as demonstrated in performance skills) and breadth of knowledge in historical and humanistic studies." Course requirements usually take 2 full-time semesters, exclusive of remedial courses.

INDIANA offers the M.A. and M.M. in musicology, the M.M. in music history and literature, and the M.M. in music history and literature with concentration in Latin-American music. Each program is outlined in great detail.

WASHINGTON: At least 45 credits (quarter system), including 9 for thesis. Also required as part of the 45 credits: methods of musical research, 3 music history courses, 3 seminars in historical musicology, 2 theory courses, 9 credits of electives.

CHICAGO: The M.A. at the University of Chicago that corresponds to the usual M.A. in musicology is in the "History and Theory of Music." 18 courses at the appropriate graduate level, including one course in bibliography, 2 in analysis, 3 in the notation and history of music to 1400, 3 in the notation and history of music from 1400 to 1700, and 3 in the history of music from 1700 to the present. "Students will normally take as their free elective one seminar each quarter during their Scholastic Residence [essentially the period of course work]. With the permission of the Graduate Advisor, students may take courses outside of the Department of Music [at the appropriate graduate level] that will be counted toward the Master's degree. . . .

"Students are expected to be able to perform creditably on some instrument or to sing, and candidates for the M.A. degree are encouraged to participate in one or more of the performance organizations on campus supported by the Department of Music. . . .

"Special fellowship funds are available for students who wish to continue private lessons with a teacher of their choice."

MICHIGAN (historical musicology): a minimum of 30 semester hours; at least 12 in either historical musicology or ethnomusicology and 8 in other musical topics. 2 courses of at least 2 hours each in a cognate field; with special approval these can be in performance. 2 courses outside the School of Music are required of the M.A. candidate if he or she plans to continue for the Ph.D. The most fundamental courses include bibliography, analysis, and certain courses in European music history, American music history, or ethnomusicology.

55

MICHIGAN (ethnomusicology): a minimum of 30 semester hours, based on studies in musicology, anthropology, linguistics, area studies, or possibly other areas, such as sociology; part of the 30 hours is a thesis (as opposed to the "critical-bibliographical essay" required in historical musicology). Qualified students may pursue an interdisciplinary degree. While performance experience is available in gamelan, Japanese ensembles, and other groups, the program concentrates on theory and method. The program is administered through the Department of Music History and Musicology, but it may also be offered in departments outside music with the cooperation of the ethnomusicologists in the School of Music, and with degree requirements being set by the department or school involved. Courses required: Introduction to graduate study; the music of Africa, South American Oceania; Euro-American folk and popular music; the music of Asia; ethnomusicology seminar; thesis. (Each counts 3 hours, except thesis, which is 2–6.)

UBC (historical musicology): At least 15 units (a typical graduate course is 1.5 units). Required: one course in bibliography and research techniques, one in analytical techniques, one in directed individual studies (may be repeated for credit); three period seminars; the remainder, other than thesis, chosen from other period seminars, one nonmusic elective, 20th-century tonal analysis, theory teaching methods, performance (maximum one unit for credit), performance practice, early notation, ethnomusicology, advanced studies in music history and musicology, topics in history of theory, theoretical studies in 20th-century music; plus thesis (3–6 units, but with no more than 3 units included in the total of 15).

UBC (ethnomusicology): At least 16 units. Required: one course in bibliography and research techniques, three in ethnomusicology (general aspects and bibliography, readings in world music cultures, transcription and analysis); one seminar in organology; ethnic music performance (maximum one unit for credit); three units of cognate electives; one music cognate or additional cognate in the arts; plus thesis (same credit as in historical musicology).

NYU: ". . .the curriculum is research oriented; most courses are concerned with extending the boundaries of current knowledge. It is designed for the professionally minded student who plans a career combining college-level teaching with continuing musicological research." For the M.A., a minimum of 36 points; required courses are proseminar in musicological research and bibliography, or style analysis, or an equivalent course, and introduction to ethnomusicology, plus at least one course concerned with each of these periods: before 1600, 1600–1800, 1800–present.

MARYLAND: "A major in musicology requires the study of musical styles and literature and of research materials in music. . . . The concentration in ethnomusicology examines the history of global music in area studies, seminars, and qualitative interdisciplinary approaches. Field work training and internships can be arranged." For the M.M., a minimum of 30 semester hours. Required: seminar in music research, early notation, and at least one graduate ethnomusicology course other than a non-Western performance ensemble.

SUNY STONY BROOK: 30 graduate credit hours, plus "Compositional Skills of Tonal Music" and "Practicum in Teaching." The 30 hours must include proseminar in tonal analysis (exemption possible by examination), 20th-century music, and 2 courses in special topics.

IOWA: "The programs offered by the Musicology area are designed to prepare students for careers in teaching, research, publishing and criticism." For the M.A., at least 37 semester hours. Required: introduction to musicology (3 hours); 20th-century analysis (3); one elective from counterpoint, musical forms, analysis of Baroque music, analysis of Classic music, analysis of Romantic music, analysis of 20th-century music, special topics in analysis, chant (3); 2 semesters of seminar in musicology (6); 2 semesters of advanced history and literature of music if dictated by the results of the advisory examination (if not so dictated, 2 period courses are substituted) (6); 2 electives in musicology (6); participation in a major performing ensemble, for academic credit, during each semester of residence (4); private lessons in performance, for academic credit (4); musicology colloquium, registered like other courses but for zero academic credit, during each semester of residence (0); thesis (2).

BERKELEY: "Students in the History and Literature program gain skills for historical research while developing a sense of critical enquiry and intellectual independence. The M.A. program introduces students to musicological methods and techniques and at the same time seeks to broaden their horizons through a variety of courses, including analysis and ethnomusicology. . . . Students in ethnomusicology explore the intellectual history of the field and study several of the world's musical traditions. . . . An unusual feature of the program, and a major advantage for students at Berkeley, is the number and variety of courses in which they are given employment and in which they teach under faculty supervision." Course requirements are "not rigidly prescribed." For the M.A. the general requirement is 24 units, at least 12 of which must be in courses admitting only graduate students. In History and Literature, these must include introduction to musical scholarship, one of the two semesters of theory and methodology in ethnomusicology, a course in analysis, and one or more proseminars in music history. In Ethnomusicology, these must include introduction to musical scholarship, both semesters of theory and methodology in ethnomusicology, a course in analysis (Western music), and one proseminar or topics course in ethnomusicology. No later than the end of the second semester in residence, the ethnomusicology major must choose "a field for research throughout the M.A. course work."

NC: Graduate work in musicology is designed mainly for students interested in study and research, an understanding of the place of music in the humanities, and teaching. For the M.A., in addition to the course in "Advanced Musicianship" mentioned on page 51, a course in resources and methods is required; other course requirements are apparently determined in consultation with an advisor. "M.A. and Ph.D. candidates may optionally include courses from other departments that may be organized as a formal minor (9 hours for the M.A., 15 hours for the Ph.D.) or as a 'supporting program'; such programs are devised and approved through consultation with the student's advisor and the departments concerned."

UNT: 32 semester hours minimum. Required: seminar in musicology (3 hours); analysis of pre-1900 music (3); 12 hours selected (with precautions against lopsidedness) from 3-hour courses in concerto literature, chamber music literature, choral literature, American music, symphonic literature, opera literature, criticism and aesthetics, history of instruments, modern harmony (12); principles of music research (3); music bibliography (3); collegium musicum (2); thesis (6).

STANFORD: 36 units minimum.

PENN: "The programs in the history of music and theory of music are closely interconnected. Students uncertain in which of these two areas they may wish to concentrate may opt for one or the other as late as the end of their first year of study without delaying their progress toward the Ph.D. degree. . . . At the Master's level, students select courses essentially from two types of offerings: proseminars and topical seminars. The proseminars deal largely (but not exclusively) with methods of scholarly research. The approaches and problems surveyed therein include the nature of evidence, text criticism, authenticity, codicology, the interpretation of theoretical treatises, criticism, hermeneutics, historiography, and musical notation. Topical seminars often have less of a methodological orientation and reflect, instead, the problems most current in a particular instructor's research." Required: 4 proseminars chosen from introduction to research, studies in musical sources, history of theory, aesthetics and criticism, historiography, early notation; 2 courses in analysis; one "Master's essay" (or an elective in its place if the student is permitted to go directly to the Ph.D. without getting an M.A.); 2 topical seminars in history or theory of music; one course of individual study or any other graduate course in the department or the university; and 2 courses of "guided reading in preparation for the comprehensive examination."

PENN's 2 courses in "guided reading" are the only evidence, in the universities surveyed, of actual degree credit assigned to the task of preparing for the master's comprehensive examination or its equivalent. In other descriptions of that examination it is emphasized that the student is being tested on what she has synthesized for herself.

WESLEYAN: The curricula in World Music leading to the M.A. and Ph.D. degrees "are created in the context of several traditions (African, Afro-American, American Indian, Indonesian, European and Euro-American, avant garde, South Indian) and several approaches (musicology, performance, theory, anthropology)." For the M.A., residence for a minimum of 2 years. Careful control of the individual's program by an individual advisor and committee. "Each student must declare one or two concentrations from the following upon entrance: (A) scholarship (ethnomusicology, musicology); (B) performance (jazz and traditional music; non-Western music; Western music); (C) experimental music/composition. Each concentration requires a set of seminars and performance courses, at least one foreign language and the completion of an M.A. thesis. During this time at least nine courses must be successfully completed. An oral exam completes the requirements, signaling acceptance of the thesis."

Required reading knowledge of foreign languages for the Master's degree

MICHIGAN: In historical musicology, one foreign language, but 2 required as part of M.A. work if the student expects to proceed to the doctorate; in ethnomusicology, French, German, or a thesis-related

59

language. Language requirements may be met by standardized examinations or by course elections. "Electing beginning language courses at Michigan, which can add from a term to a year to your program, is expensive and time consuming, and it is not a good use of your time at the University." SUNY STONY BROOK: French and German. "The German examination must be taken at the beginning of the first semester of study. Both examinations must have been taken by the second semester." TORONTO: German and either French, Italian, or Latin. WASHINGTON: German, French, Italian, or Latin. STANFORD: French, German, or Italian. CLAREMONT: German, French, or Italian. "It is recommended that the examinations be completed before the end of the first semester of graduate study. Intensive language-study classes are usually offered in the Claremont Summer Session." INDIANA: German, "by the end of one calendar year of enrollment." "In exceptional circumstances additional or substitute languages may be required."

NC: A departmental examination in one modern foreign language. WISCONSIN: One foreign language. "Foreign language competency should be satisfied by the end of the second semester." UBC: German or French. BERKELEY: Written examination with dictionary, in French or German. "Students are expected to work on a language every semester until they pass the examination." MARYLAND: "A reading knowledge of one pertinent foreign language, preferably German, is required and must be demonstrated early in the first semester of residence. A student may not pursue the degree program beyond one year nor request Comprehensive Examinations without fulfilling the reading proficiency." COLUMBIA: In historical musicology, translation examinations in German and in Latin or French; in ethnomusicology, translation examinations in German and French. IOWA: French or German, passed before the Master's final examination. NYU: Reading proficiency in German (preferably) or in either French or Italian, demonstrated during the first term of graduate study. PENN: German and either French or Italian. "In special circumstances, another language may be substituted for French or Italian." WESLEYAN: See page 59.

CHICAGO: For the M.A. in the history and theory of music (see page 55), "two foreign languages, one of which must be German. Candidates who wish to continue their studies for the Ph.D. are strongly urged to complete their language requirements as soon as possible." "Language examinations are administered by the Department of Music to its students. Students do not take the Foreign Language Reading Examinations administered by the University.

"Departmental examinations are given each quarter, except summer, and are announced several weeks in advance. These examinations require the student to translate about 400 words of a passage of medium difficulty from source materials or musicological literature. Students are given two hours to translate the entire passage with the aid of a dictionary; the quality as well as the accuracy of the translation are judged. Sample examinations are available in the Department office.

"Satisfactory progress in the Department includes passing one language examination per year. . . . Students who meet or exceed this expectation are given preference in consideration of financial aid. Students are urged whenever possible to complete their language requirements before they enter Research Residence [i.e., before completion of the main body of course work]."

General examinations and evaluations; other requirements

IOWA: Before the end of the second semester in residence, the student must pass an examination in the history and literature of music and present suitable samples of scholarly research and writing. At or near the end of course work there is a final examination, either written or oral or both. NYU: A general examination that also serves as the qualifying examination for the doctorate. NC: A final oral examination on coursework; there is no final written examination. "At the beginning of each spring semester a qualifying examination is given to those who wish to proceed to the Ph.D. program after finishing the M.A. Students already in the Department's M.A. program will be advised to take the examination in the second year. Those who received the M.A. at another institution must take the examination in the spring of the first year of study; these students will be evaluated during the second semester of study and advised as to whether they should continue."

SUNY STONY BROOK: "Written and oral examinations in the history of music and in the analysis of preassigned compositions." MARYLAND: "[Written] Comprehensive Examinations as prescribed by the music faculty are required of all master's degree students as they near completion of the degree requirements." PENN: A written comprehensive examination in the history and theory of music, serving as both the final examination for the M.A. and the preliminary examination for "doctoral candidacy." COLUMBIA: In historical musicology, a written examination on music history and style; in ethnomusicology, no general examination. INDIANA: The master's examination in musicology for the M.M. or the M.A. is taken toward the end of the completion of course work. Passing it entitles the student to apply for admission to the Ph.D. program.

MICHIGAN: In historical musicology, a comprehensive examination during the Fall term of the second year on major works of Western music, based on scores and recorded examples. The student intending to pursue the Ph.D. is evaluated near the end of M.A. work. A M.A. from elsewhere who has nominally begun the Ph.D. program is evaluated "at the end of the first term of residence on the basis of performance in course work during that term and on the master's comprehensive examination and essay. The department's judgment is a collective one. If this evaluation is favorable, the student may continue in the Ph.D. program." In ethnomusicology, there is no comprehensive examination (but note on page 63 how thesis requirements differ in ethnomusicology and historical musicology).

BERKELEY: (1) A short oral examination on a composition assigned 24 hours earlier (more time is allowed if transcription is required); (2) a 3-hour written examination. If in history and literature of music, it tests specific and synoptic knowledge of music from various periods or cultural areas; if in ethnomusicology, it tests advancement in "ethnomusicological study," and is based on the field chosen for research. TORONTO: See page 69. CLAREMONT: "The written examination includes aspects of the student's course work. . . . The oral examination includes the identification of musical examples."

CHICAGO: A "general examination in the History and Theory of Music. This is given at the end of the quarter in which the candidate completes the required courses for the degree, usually at the end of Scholastic Residence [the main body of course work]. Based upon the examination, as well as upon general performance within the M.A. program, the Department will determine whether a student who passes the examination will be accepted into the Ph.D. program. . . .

"The M.A.—and Ph.D. qualifying—examination in the History and Theory of Music is normally administered over three days during exam week in the Spring Quarter. The examination will consist of the following:

"1. A written examination of approximately six hours on the student's knowledge of the history of music. The student will be asked to write three two-hour essays in each of the following periods: (a)

Music to 1600, (b) Music from 1600 to 1800, and (c) Music from 1800 to the present. There will be a choice of topics. . . .

"2. A written examination of approximately three hours on the student's knowledge of music literature. The usual format for this examination is as twelve "singlesheets" of music. The student is asked to identify the excerpts as closely as possible, to arrange them in chronological order, and to discuss the reasons for the identifications and chronology in considerable detail. . . .

"3. A written analysis of a major composition, to be completed within 24 hours. A choice between two compositions is often given. . . .

"4. An oral evaluation and discussion of the written examination with the faculty. . . ."

Thesis or final document

Back to the question of whether an American master's thesis ought to resemble the Ph.D. in being an original contribution to knowledge, or whether it ought to resemble the baccalaureate degree in being essentially an advanced certificate of knowledge attained. IOWA, WASHINGTON, and MARYLAND seem to believe the former; most of the other institutions surveyed apparently hold to the latter. The experience at IOWA and MARYLAND has often been that despite all urgings for brevity the master's thesis gets out of control and goes on forever. One reads between the lines of NC's statement that it is the nature of the thesis beast to require precisely engineered restraints. Other statements are careful to describe the thesis as an expanded research paper and no more. MICHIGAN construes a formal thesis as a basic element in its ethnomusicology M.A., and something not as basic for its M.A. in historical musicology. CHICAGO presumably requires enough research and writing in the rest of its curriculum to consider a master's thesis superfluous.

CHICAGO: None.

USC: A comprehensive examination, usually during the last semester of course work, instead of a thesis.

YALE: A "major project" as outgrowth of one of the 8 courses in the one-year M.A. program; the course is taken in the second semester of residence, and may be taught tutorially. NYU: An approved paper representing the student's best work. COLUMBIA: In historical musicology, a thesis in the form of 2 essays that may have been begun as term papers; in ethnomusicology, a thesis, or 2 essays that may have been begun as term papers.

PENN: "Candidates for the A.M. degree submit an article-length essay. Students admitted to doctoral candidacy may bypass the A.M. degree (and the essay requirement) with the permission of the faculty." The A.M. essay must be presented at "a departmental colloquium or other appropriate forum." MICHIGAN: In ethnomusicology, a formal thesis for 2–6 semester hours of credit. In historical musicology, a critical-bibliographical essay "reviewing the state of research on a musical topic selected by the student. A selective bibliography should be included, but the heart of the paper is intended to be a prose description of the extent and quality of information available on the topic." The paper should show what still needs to be done and demonstrate the student's ability to work independently. Due on the last Monday in September in the second year of residence. STANFORD: "An investigative essay." SUNY STONY BROOK: "A substantial essay, normally one which the student has written as part of the coursework, is required. The paper should be submitted no later than the third week of the semester in which the student expects to receive the degree."

NC: The thesis "must derive from a paper prepared for a graduate course." The student signs up for thesis in the fourth semester of residence; it is required that the thesis be completed in that semester. The work is done as in any other independent study course; the thesis course "will meet every week or every other week, at the discretion of the instructor. The goal of the course will be to revise (but not significantly expand) a paper written in a previous course, normally a course taught by the thesis advisor. (A student will not begin a totally new work as a thesis.)" The thesis is graded with letter grades, not with an "S." The graduate calendar must be followed, which means that the date of completion must be about a month before the end of the semester. An incomplete grade is granted only with a letter of application to the director of graduate studies, endorsed by the thesis advisor; the incomplete grade has to be removed in the following semester by a date fixed by the thesis advisor.

WESLEYAN: The thesis "can follow a great many formats and modes of musical investigation; performance per se does not constitute a thesis without ancillary materials."

IOWA: The thesis topic is presented in preliminary form to the musicology faculty "as soon as possible after the first year of study."

After the general topic is approved and an advisor is assigned by the mutual consent of student and faculty, a very detailed proposal is written. At completion a defense is required. WASHINGTON: Within the first 2 weeks of the 4th quarter of graduate study, "the student must submit a thesis topic in the form of a working title and substantial memorandum explaining the objectives, methods, and materials proposed. . . . The actual writing . . . is usually postponed until all, or most, of the required course work is completed. The time to be allowed for the writing should be determined in consultation with the Adviser. . . . The completed draft of the thesis, in proper form, must be submitted for a first reading by the Supervisory Committee not later than the beginning (first two weeks) of the ninth quarter of graduate study. . . ." The final examination on the M.A. thesis is oral. MARYLAND: A thesis given 6 hours of course credit and traditionally equivalent, in effort required, to two graduate courses, culminating in a formal oral examination that emphasizes but is not limited to the topic of the thesis.

Requirements for the M.Phil. Degree in Musicology at Columbia

Among the institutions surveyed, only COLUMBIA offers the M. Phil. in musicology as a degree separately described, even though its graduate school, like the graduate schools of CUNY, KANSAS, and possibly other institutions, confers the M. Phil. as a matter of course, or upon request, to Ph.D. students who have been admitted to candidacy (those for whom only the dissertation remains). (KANSAS: "The degree is not granted automatically, but may be requested by students in approved programs who feel that the degree will assist them in undertakings prior to completion of the Doctor of Philosophy degree.") No doubt one reason Columbia goes into such detail on the M. Phil. in musicology is that its dissertation requirement may be satisfied not only in the usual way but also by any body of published work in the field deemed significant enough by the faculty. Thus for some students at Columbia the M. Phil. may be considered an appropriate preparation for professional accomplishment in the world outside the campus. All the information following in this section, then, pertains to Columbia.

Course requirements

30 points of courses beyond the M.A. degree, chosen in consultation with the advisor. In historical musicology, courses must include 4 semesters of seminars in historical musicology at the highest graduate level, e.g., seminars in historical periods, musical aesthetics, the phenomenology of music, the history of theory, ethnomusicology, composition, music librarianship. In ethnomusicology, courses must include 2 semesters of early notation or any 2 semesters of historical musicology at the highest level, 2 semesters of seminar in field methods and techniques, and 2 semesters of advanced seminar in ethnomusicology. In ethnomusicology with a specialization in music theory, courses must include those required for ethnomusicology plus 2 semesters of proseminar in music theory and 4 semesters of upper-level theory seminars.

Required reading knowledge of foreign languages

In historical musicology: a translation examination in French or Latin if not passed at the M.A. level, or in a language or languages related to the dissertation. The student's native language will not fulfill the requirement. In ethnomusicology: French, German, and a third language related to the topic of specialization.

Field work in ethnomusicology

A minimum of one year of field work appropriate to the topic of specialization.

General examinations and evaluations

In historical musicology: a written examination on a special field chosen by the student, with interpretation of documents in the required languages. Students beginning the M. Phil. with an M.A. from another institution must take the departmental M.A. examination in historical musicology, and must submit samples of their scholarly writing. In ethnomusicology: a written examination, 1/3 on the history of Western art music, 1/3 on general ethnomusicology, 1/3 on special ethnomusicology; also an oral examination.

Requirements for the Ph.D. Degree in Musicology

Course and residence requirements, timetables, advisement

ALL: The curriculum must be chosen with the guidance of one or more faculty advisors.

ALL: There are provisions for modifying or waiving certain requirements in unusual circumstances.

COLUMBIA: See the preceding section.

USC: "In addition to the 30 units for the M.A. in music history and literature, a minimum of 26 units of course work is required [plus the dissertation.] Students should consult their guidance committees to devise appropriate courses of study."

PRINCETON: "Courses offered by the musicology faculty make no attempt to cover all musics or the entire range of Western music or musical theory. Since the faculty believes that students will learn most about the nature and methods of musicological inquiry by pursuing it, rather than reading about it, the courses mostly deal with fields in which faculty members are actively engaged. . . .

"Most of the graduate courses are conducted as seminars, ranging in size from three or four to eight or 10 students. The typical seminar proceeds by a combination of lecture, discussion, and student presentation of original work. . . .

"Students at all stages are expected to carry on independent study and research. Advice from faculty members is available to them at all times."

SUNY STONY BROOK: "A plan of study in the form of a working contract toward candidacy will be drawn up jointly by the student and a directing committee early in the student's first semester. The Directing Committee will consist of the student's advisor and at least two other faculty members. . . .

"The design of the program is to be developed around . . . [the required portion], and the contract should specify such terms as the core of courses to be taken, the length of full-time residence, and the schedule and subject areas of various examinations including the preliminary examination. The terms of the contract should be completed within one or two years [beyond the master's degree], depending upon the scope of the program."

SUNY STONY BROOK'S "contract toward candidacy" requires "a number of essays [which may have been written as coursework] demonstrating proficiency in various aspects of musicological research, theoretical studies, analysis or criticism"; an essay on 20th-century music; a public lecture or colloquium on 20th-century music; the teaching of at least 2 semester courses, "at least one of which shall be an introductory college course in musicianship, theory or literature"; a seminar in the teaching of music, including the presentation of at least one project or report; plus foreign languages, preliminary examination, and dissertation.

YALE: The traditional preparation is for careers as scholars and teachers in institutions of higher learning, and also for work in music criticism, music publishing, the recording industry. Ph.D. work should develop methods of inquiry, critical judgment, skepticism and curiosity. Most students will do some undergraduate teaching at Yale. The Ph.D. program lasts 4–5 years beyond the baccalaureate, or 6 years if the dissertation requires research abroad. The residence requirement is a minimum of 3 years. The usual schedule is 2 years of course work, a summer of preparation for the Ph.D. qualifying examination (which is taken early in the third year), and 2–3 more years of dissertation plus teaching.

"Each year Yale College employs a number of graduate students as Teaching Fellows and Acting Instructors in order to offer smaller classes and more individual instruction than would otherwise be possible, given the limited size of the faculty. The practice of employing graduate students as teachers has mutual benefits: it allows the College to offer the best possible instruction to Yale undergraduates in the face of limited economic resources, and it gives teaching experience and financial support to the graduate student."

The Ph.D. must normally be completed within 6 years. In the first year all students take 4 courses per semester. Usually this is continued at the same rate in the second year (with possible variations according to past training and present progress), so that the standard is 16 courses. In addition the Ph.D. student takes a research seminar in each semester before the qualifying examination. Accommodation to past training does not take place until the second year; in the first year all students are in essentially the same program regardless of background.

At Yale there is no fixed schedule of graduate courses. The schedule varies according to the faculty's research interests and the students' needs. Certain basic courses (for instance, tonal analysis, seminar in the Romantic era) are offered at least every other year. In each semester at least 7 graduate courses are given: 3 in music history, 3 in music theory, one in theory and aesthetics. The schedule is determined by the Graduate Curriculum Committee.

Each May the faculty discusses the progress of each student in the first and second year, recommending schedule adjustments, dates of qualifying examinations, removal of students from the program, admission to candidacy (normally at the end of the second year), and so forth. A student not admitted to candidacy is not allowed to register for the third year.

STANFORD: "The Ph.D. requires a minimum of three years of full-time work [beyond the master's]. The student may proceed directly to the Ph.D. without taking the M.A. en route." "In keeping with the department's philosophy of fostering well-rounded musicianship within the framework of a university education, many of the department's Ph.D. candidates are active as performers."

TORONTO: Since it would be misleading to divide Toronto's program description into isolated categories, the following quotations are given verbatim and are cross-referenced in other sections of the present survey.

"Both the M.A. and the Ph.D. programs offer instruction in all areas of historical musicology. While ethnomusicology is not an independent course of study, instruction is offered at the graduate level, and Ph.D. candidates may choose to specialize in some aspect of non-Western music. In addition, area studies may be done outside the department, notably in the Department of East Asian Studies. Interdisciplinary studies are likewise possible in the Centre for Medieval Studies and the Centre for the Study of Drama.

"Three full courses and a three-part comprehensive examination are required to complete the one-year M.A. program. All candidates must satisfy departmental requirements in German and one of French, Italian or Latin before graduation. The Ph.D. requires an additional year of course work beyond the M.A. [three additional full courses], followed by a [comprehensive and] major field examination. A third language must be offered beyond those required for the M.A. This third language will normally be determined by the requirements of the major field of study. The thesis is defended at a final oral examination."

HARVARD: "...musicology is broadly defined as the disciplined study of music, and includes the historical, comparative, and systematic aspects of the field. The primary emphasis within the program is on the history, theory, and literature of Western music, from antiquity to the present. Advanced studies are also available in ethnomusicology. Most graduate courses in musicology are research seminars on specific topics and deal with current problems in the field. On the completion of preparatory training and the passing of the General and Oral Examinations, Ph.D. dissertations may be written in any one of these fields. . . .

"Since teaching is an integral part of graduate training, most graduate students are Teaching Fellows during part of the time they are at Harvard."

A total of 16 "half-courses" are taken for the Ph.D., 2 of which must be in theory or composition. 14 are usually taken in the first 2 years. Up to 8 are transferable for credit from other graduate schools, "subject to evaluation by the Department and acceptance by the Graduate School. Petitions may be submitted after the completion of one full year of graduate work in the Department." "The third year is primarily devoted to developing a dissertation proposal and the beginning of work on the dissertation. All students will take at least two more half courses, the topics of which may be assigned by the faculty as a result of the General Examination."

"The progress of all graduate students is reviewed at the end of each year. In addition to adequate course work, there are special requirements for first and second year students. Every student must submit at least one paper written for a graduate course as part of the first year review. Musicology students must take an analysis exam. . . ." In the first 2 years, satisfactory progress is required for permission to register. A prospective third-year student must have at least a B average and must have passed general examinations. A prospective fourth-year student must have dissertation approval. "A prospective sixth-year, or more advanced, student must have produced at least one acceptable chapter of the dissertation or its equivalent for each year beginning with the fifth."

WEST VIRGINIA: "The general progress of every student shall be evaluated at the end of each academic year by the Committee on Graduate Studies or its designates. If a student is judged to be 'off schedule'. . . the Director of Graduate Studies will review his overall record. If some corrective action is judged necessary, recommendation for such action will be made to the Committee on Graduate Studies after a conference with the student. . . . The student will be given opportunity to . . . request that action be reconsidered. . . .

"Action taken by the Committee on Graduate Studies may range from unconditional restoration of a status of satisfactory progress, to the withdrawal of financial support or assistantship, to the termination of the student's registration in the program. Normally, however, a probationary period of not more than two semesters will be set during which the student must meet the conditions specified for full restoration of a status of satisfactory progress. All actions taken by the committee on graduate studies will be expressed to the student in writing."

NYU: Most courses are concerned with extending current knowledge through research. For the professionally minded student who will become part of academia as teacher and scholar. At least 3 years of full-time study (72 points) past the baccalaureate, at least one year of which must be in residence. All requirements must be completed not later than 10 years from the date of matriculation, or 7 years if the student holds the master's degree at the time of admission. Historical musicology: Courses required are proseminar in musicological research and bibliography, or style analysis, or an equivalent course, and introduction to musicology, plus at least one course in music before 1600, one in music from 1600 to 1800, and one in music from 1800 to the present, plus a course in early notation and a course in theory and analysis.

Ethnomusicology: The program is planned in consultation with the director of graduate studies and the coordinator of the ethnomusicology program.

COLORADO: 30 hours of course work beyond the master's, and also "a minimum of thirty hours of dissertation credits. . . ." WASHINGTON: 27 credits of course work beyond the master's, plus 27 credits minimum for the dissertation.

CLAREMONT: "The Ph.D. in Musicology requires a minimum of 72 units beyond the bachelor's degree.

Work completed towards the M.A. degree in Music at The Claremont Graduate School may be used as partial satisfaction of this requirement at the rate of 12 units per semester up to a total of 30 units. Students transferring to The Claremont Graduate School from other accredited graduate institutions may request the transfer of a maximum of 24 units of appropriate work earned elsewhere." The 42 units beyond the 30 for the M.A. are: historical era courses emphasizing performance practice, 16; performance (or composition, with permission), 4; electives, 4–8; dissertation, 10–6; non-music minor, all in one field, 8.

BERKELEY: Ph.D. training is traditionally for university and college teaching, sometimes for editing, criticism, arts management. As compared with training for the M.A., it "involves more detailed work in research seminars and special studies." The Ph.D. usually takes about 5 years past the baccalaureate; students are encouraged to go as fast as they can. The residence requirement is satisfied by taking at least 4 units of appropriate graduate courses for at least 2 years. Most Ph.D. students enter directly from the Berkeley M.A.; such students might expect to finish course work, supplementary requirements, the dissertation prospectus, and the qualifying examination by the end of 2 years if they are in historical musicology; ethnomusicology will probably take longer. Then the student is advanced to doctoral candidacy, at which point only the dissertation remains. The minimum grade-point average is 3.5; additional work may be prescribed if that average is not maintained in seminars.

As with its M.A. program (see pages 57–58), "a major advantage for students at Berkeley. . .is the number and variety of courses in which they are given employment and in which they teach under faculty supervision. Teaching experience of this kind is both a philosophical and practical aim of the program and a means of student employment." "Doctoral students are required to serve as Graduate Student Instructors for at least one academic year."

Required in history and literature: 2 courses in supervised independent study, a course introducing musical scholarship, one of the two semesters of theory and methodology in ethnomusicology, a course in analysis, one or more proseminars in music history, at least 4 semesters of research seminars, and a course in fugue or composition. Required in ethnomusicology: 2 courses in supervised independent study, introduction to musical scholarship, both semesters of theory and methodology in ethnomusicology, a course in analysis (Western music), one proseminar or topics course in ethnomusicology, at least 2 semesters of seminars, and "pertinent course work in related disciplines."

"Performance plays an important part in the life of the Department, and graduate students are strongly encouraged to take part in it."

KANSAS: "Specific course work for each student will be arranged individually in consultation with the director of the division of music history. . . . The Ph.D. program will normally require a minimum of three years of full-time study beyond the master's degree, with the first two years devoted to course work and the third year to the dissertation. . . ." Required: At least 2 semesters of collegium musicum and 2 semesters of seminar in music history.

"Although the Ph.D. program does not include a minor area, students are encouraged to continue their study of performance and/or composition, and may be advised to take courses in other related fields that are directly applicable to their chosen fields or research for the dissertation. . . .

"Each student for the Ph.D. degree program in music must have a minimum of one semester of teaching experience in his or her field before completing the degree. This requirement can be satisfied either by filling a regular faculty position at a college or university or by supervised teaching at the University of Kansas on a teaching assistant-ship. . . .

"Each candidate for the Ph.D. degree in music will be required to make a public presentation of no less than 20 minutes on a scholarly topic. This requirement may be fulfilled by reading a paper at a national or regional meeting of a society in the student's discipline or in a colloquium at the University of Kansas."

WASHINGTON: "The degree requirements in both the M.A. and Ph.D. programs focus largely upon the acquisition of knowledge and the development of skills in independent investigation. The student should not, however, neglect those aspects of performance and general musicianship which represent his most basic professional credentials. It is recommended that the student involve himself continuously with active music making, as in the further development of proficiency and artistry in his own performance field, participation in ensembles, attendance at rehearsals and concerts, and so on. Maintenance of professional skills is often an important consideration in the securing of employment after the award of an advanced degree."

CUNY GRADUATE CENTER: 3 or more years full-time (at least 60 credits) beyond the bachelor's degree. At least 30 credits must be taken in residence (full-time residence is at least 12 credits per semester). Up to 30 credits of equivalent courses may be transferred from another institution. Required of students entering with a B.A. only: 4 proseminars (one in bibliography, 2 in music history, one in theory/analysis), 7 research seminars, 2 courses in early notation, one course in ethnomusicology, 6 electives.

At least 30 credits beyond the master's degree (same full-time residence requirement), including 5 research seminars, one course in early notation, one course in ethnomusicology, and 3 electives. Courses at the master's level should have included bibliography, style analysis, 2 music history seminars, and one course in early notation; these have to be made up in addition to the 30 credits if they were not taken.

UNT: 90 semester hours beyond the bachelor's, 60 hours beyond the UNT master's. A master's from an accredited institution will usually be accepted for the first 30 hours. At least 60 hours at UNT. A maximum of 30 hours of equivalent courses may be transferred for degree credit. The minimum residence requirement is at least 2 semesters, in each of which at least 9 semester hours of courses applicable to the degree are taken. The degree must be completed within 10 years.

"Upon completion of the first semester of graduate study, the student should fill out a 'Request for Designation of Advisory Committee,' available in the Office of Graduate Studies in Music. An advisory committee, consisting of the major professor, minor professor, and one other faculty member, will be tentatively approved by the Director of Graduate Studies in Music. The request will then be forwarded to the Deans of the School of Music and the Graduate School for final approval. The student should then arrange to meet with his/her major professor for assistance in working out a degree plan."

Course requirements beyond the UNT master's are the following; presumably some courses in addition to the 60 hours might need to be taken by holders of master's degrees from elsewhere. Seminar in musicology, 6 hours; early notation, 6; courses in the music literature of the medieval, Renaissance, Baroque, Classical, Romantic, or modern periods, 12; from among courses in the Beethoven quartets, Wagner, or history of theory, 6; electives in music, 3–6; collegium musicum, 3; electives in minor or related fields, 9–12; dissertation, 12; total, 60.

IOWA: 73 hours beyond the bachelor's. The usual residence and transfer-credit rules. The curriculum listed here for the Ph.D. incorporates the Iowa M.A. curriculum; an accredited M.A. from elsewhere is accepted, although that student might have to take some courses in addition to the 73 hours. Contemporary analysis and theory, 3 hours; theory electives, 6; lessons in performance, 6; electives outside musicology, anywhere in the university, 3; introduction to musicology, 3; seminar in musicology, taken 5 times, 15; advanced bibliography, 4; early notation, 3; physics of music, 3; required attendance at musicology colloquium, zero credit but registered like any other course, 0; advanced history and literature, 6; 5 musicology electives, 15; M.A. thesis, 2 (if the

M.A. is from another university, major research papers are substituted); Ph.D. thesis, 4; total, 73.

UT AT AUSTIN: "The scholarly study of music embodied in the Ph.D. program in music in the area of musicology has as one aim the knowledge of Western music in its historical and cultural context. It is also concerned with the historiography and systematic aspects of the discipline itself. What the program attempts to do is to acquaint the student not only with a body of knowledge but also with the questions, issues, problems, and lacunae which surround that knowledge—in short, with the intellectual challenges of musicological research. The program seeks to equip the student with a variety of tools, approaches, and methodologies, both theoretical and practical, for undertaking independent scholarly research and writing in the field. The faculty strongly believe that seminar courses provide the best classroom train- ing ground they can offer the doctoral student for developing both the body of knowledge and the ways of knowing that are appropriate to the Ph.D. degree in musicology. Because the degree represents an achieve- ment that is larger than the sum of its parts, completion of the minimum program outlined here cannot guarantee that a student is prepared to receive the Ph.D."

Residence requirement: 2 long-term semesters full time. "Any graduate work done at another institution is subject to validation by the musicology faculty, and courses listed on the program of work at the time of application for candidacy may not be more than six years old."

63–66 hours beyond the bachelor's, including work done for the M.M.: foundations of musicology, 3 hours; bibliography and research methods, 3; foundations of ethnomusicology, 3; advanced studies in medieval, Renaissance, Baroque, 18th-century, 19th-century, or 20th- century music, 6; seminars in the history of music, special problems in musicology and ethnomusicology, seminar in theory and composition, 12–15; one of 2 courses in history of theory, 3; one of 2 courses in early notation, 6; analytical techniques, 3; seminar in theory and composition, 3; special topics in ethnomusicology, music of the Americas, area studies in ethnomusicology, problems in performance practice, lessons in per- formance, 12; upper-division or graduate course in other departments, 3; dissertation, 6; total, 63–66.

CHICAGO: The Ph.D. at the University of Chicago that corre- sponds to the usual Ph.D. in musicology is in the "History and Theory of Music." "Ph.D. students who enter with a Bachelor's degree will register for six quarters of *Scholastic Residence*. In most cases, this will be primarily a period of course work, the number and distribution of which are set by the departments and division. In the ensuing six quarters, students will enter *Research Residence.* The precise mix of courses and independent research during this period will depend on the individual program and the student's academic progress." A normal graduate load is 3 courses.

"The degree of Doctor of Philosophy is awarded to candidates who have shown marked ability. . . . The Department will accept those students who have demonstrated their competence to work with independence and originality in the field of music."

"During each quarter of Research Residence [i.e., after the bulk of course work is complete], a Ph.D. student is required to take one seminar for a letter grade. With the permission of the Graduate Advisor, students may substitute two or three courses from outside the Department of Music . . . [at the appropriate level]. In addition, students are required to register for the Departmental Colloquium . . . .

"Students entering the program with a Master's degree from another institution are expected to enroll for one year of Scholastic Residence [the period primarily devoted to course work] before entering Research Residence. Programs of study will be worked out to meet individual needs and requirements. These students are presumed to have the training equivalent to the M.A. program at the University of Chicago, including skills in practical musicianship. Students are required to make up any deficiencies in their course work and to pass the six Practicum Examinations." (See pages 51–52.)

UBC: "The Ph.D. in Musicology is offered with emphasis on either Historical Musicology or Music Theory, with the certification of degree form reflecting this distinction." 12 units beyond the Master's in addition to Ph.D. thesis (a typical graduate course is 1.5 units; no units are assigned to thesis). A minimum of 6 units must be in historical musicology. Aside from up to three units of arts electives, only courses or seminars in these topics are allowed: advanced theory, selected topics, analytical techniques, tonal analysis in 20th-century music, topics in history of theory, theoretical studies in 20th-century music, theory teaching methods, directed individual studies, performance practice, early notation, period seminars, ethnomusicology, 20th-century music in general, advanced studies in music history and musicology, performance (maximum 2 units for credit).

WISCONSIN: "The residence requirement . . . cannot be satisfied by summer sessions or part-time attendance only. Each doctoral candidate must spend at least two semesters of full-time study in the doctoral field beyond the master's degree level, preferably within a single academic year, carrying in each of these semesters a full load of at least nine credits of graduate course work and research. Such a period of full-time reading, reflection, study, performance and research, without the distraction of outside responsibilities, is necessary to give the student continuity. . . ."

The Ph.D. is "never granted for a program of miscellaneous studies. Each program as a whole must be rationally unified and all courses must contribute to an organized program of study and research. Courses must be selected from groups embracing one principal subject of concentration, called the major; and from one or two related fields, called the minor. . . ." Required in ethnomusicology: "two semesters of bibliography and research methods; six seminars and/or courses in ethnomusicology, and at least one seminar or graduate course in music history or theory." Required in music history: music reference and research materials, proseminar in musicology, seminar in early notation, and 7 additional upper-level seminars or courses in independent research. "In Ph.D. programs a limited amount of performance study may apply toward residence credit. . . ." On the minor in ethnomusicology: ". . .an interdisciplinary minor in the respective area studies program of the student's main geographical area of interest is usually advisable. . . .

"Each graduate student's work will be reviewed every semester by the Director of Graduate Studies, the student's adviser, and the Area Committee. The Graduate Committee will receive a report each semester from the Director of Graduate Studies on the progress of all students. This review will be based on standards and requirements set forth in these criteria or in Graduate School regulations. If satisfactory progress is not being made, a signed statement from the Director of Graduate Studies and the adviser will be sent, informing the student that continuation of graduate study will not be permitted."

WESLEYAN: Two years of full-time course work, plus a two-semester thesis course; the remainder depends on advisement. "The qualification for the Ph.D. may be accomplished in several ways by agreement with the candidate's committee. The demonstration of qualification may include written or oral examination, concerts and other documented musical activity, and is concerned with both broad and specialized knowledge."

"Field work: In many cases, one full year of field work is considered to be an essential part of a Ph.D. program. The nature of the field work should be planned with the dissertation adviser and the candidate's committee."

MICHIGAN: Occasionally all requirements except the dissertation may be fulfilled in 2 years beyond the master's degree, including summers, if there are no deficiencies and if the language requirements are met upon admission. More often a third year is necessary. More time is required of students with "assistantships and other obligations that prevent them from taking full course loads. . . ." The normal doctoral load is 8–9 hours per long term (unlike the normal M.A. load at Michigan, which is 12 hours). No credit from other institutions may be transferred for doctoral degrees.

The residence requirement is at least 2 terms of full-time enrollment (taking at least 2 graduate courses carrying at least 8 hours of credit, or 6 hours if the student is a graduate assistant). "The purpose of the residence requirement at the doctoral level is to ensure that each student has ample opportunity and encouragement to participate fully in the musical life of the School of Music. This involves not only attending classes and lessons but also attending concerts, recitals, lectures, conferences, and symposia sponsored by the School as well as engaging in regular, informal exchanges with other students and faculty. . . . During the two terms of 8-hour enrollment the student must participate as an active member of the School of Music by being present in School of Music facilities (or attending School of Music classes or other activities in other University facilities) in a learning environment for a substantial period at least three days per week. In addition, the student must be approved by his or her department as having satisfied the purposes of the residence requirement. Enrollment in summer half-terms only will not satisfy the residence requirement."

Doctoral programs vary according to student interests. In historical musicology: "The student elects courses and seminars designed to deepen knowledge and refine methodology. Elections should include at least four seminars . . . and a study of the notation of early music (if not previously completed). In consultation with an academic advisor, a student should select two subject areas (such as historical periods, ethnomusicology, or American music), a sequence of three graduate courses then being elected in each subject area. The advanced doctoral student may pursue independent study . . . by submitting a written proposal to the Graduate Committee during the term prior to election.

Typically the Preliminary and Field Examinations occur during the fourth term of residence as a doctoral student." In ethnomusicology: "By the end of the second year the student [who, typically, has already earned the M.A. in ethnomusicology] should select a field of concentration." Field work is encouraged but not required. "Typically the student will begin preliminary examinations during the fourth term of residence as a doctoral student."

PENN: "Doctoral candidates have considerable flexibility in their selection of courses. They are free to take historical seminars within the department, to arrange courses of individual study with particular members of the faculty, to select courses in theory or composition, or to enroll in appropriate graduate courses outside the department. . . . Eight additional course units are required beyond the twelve required for the A.M. degree. They may consist of any graduate course or any course of individually guided research within or outside the Department of Music."

MARYLAND: A minimum of 3 years of full-time study beyond the baccalaureate; at least 30 semester hours beyond the Master's, not including dissertation; a minimum of one year of residence. "Requirements . . . include the satisfactory completion of a body of course work beyond the master's degree (no fixed number of credits) that in the judgment of the student and the Graduate Adviser adequately prepares the student for Preliminary Examinations; the successful completion of those Examinations; Admission to Candidacy; the submission of an approved dissertation; and an oral final examination in defense of the dissertation. . . ." Doctoral candidacy must be achieved within 5 years of admission, and all degree work must be completed within another 4 years.

"The core of the curriculum in musicology is historically oriented. Within each academic year, the student has an opportunity to pursue one formal approach or another to all of the traditionally defined style periods in Western culture. To complement the core, a broad range of supporting studies is selected from areas such as ethnomusicology, music theory, music analysis, individual composers and genres, early music notation, performance, and performance practice. . . . The core of the curriculum in ethnomusicology is a continuing investigation of global music and includes field work training in the Baltimore-Washington area. Course work elected at The University of Maryland Baltimore County is equally applicable to the degree. Internships with various branches of the Smithsonian Institution and the Archive of Folk Culture

(Library of Congress) are available. Area Studies and Seminars examine traditional and current scholarship with a different emphasis each semester...."

ILLINOIS: "Doctoral programs are divided into three stages." Stage I is the master's degree. Stage II: "One or more additional years devoted to course work and research in preparation for the preliminary examination, and fulfillment of the department's special requirements.... Each department has a procedure for evaluating a student's progress toward the doctorate.... Such evaluation will take place no later than the end of the second year after a student enters the Graduate College." Stage III is the dissertation. Time limit for the doctorate is 7 years past the bachelor's.

"The Ph.D. in musicology is intended for those whose interests lie in research in the history of music, systematic musicology, or ethnomusicology." A minimum of 16 units beyond the master's degree, including at least 2 units in the seminar in musicology. 8 of the 16 are for the dissertation. "Although no formal outside minor is required, students are expected to take courses in fields outside music that are appropriate to the proposed area of thesis research."

INDIANA: The Ph.D. "represents breadth of experience and training in the arts and sciences and is recommended for those planning to enter a field involving research or scholarly writing as well as college teaching in musicology, music theory, or music education." Minimum of 90 hours for the Ph.D., including the master's degree, at least 30 of which must have been completed at Indiana. "In the event that a student wishes to bypass the master's degree, the first 30 hours of graduate work will be considered the equivalent of the master's degree and will be subject to the requirements and regulations that apply to the master's degree." "All doctoral students . . . are required to complete two 12-hour minors. The first of these minors is within the School of Music, the second is in an area inside or outside the School of Music."

The musicology Ph.D. may be in either historical musicology or performance practice. Indiana's announcement describes each of these programs in considerable detail.

"Final admission to the curriculum is contingent on passing the Major Field Examination in Musicology, which must be taken during the first regular semester of enrollment. . . . No more than 9 hours beyond the master's degree requirements taken before passing the Major Field Exam may be applied toward the Ph.D. in musicology. An applicant who has passed the Master's Examination in Musicology at Indiana University and who has been recommended by the faculty for admission to the Ph.D. curriculum is exempted from taking the Major Field Exam."

Required reading knowledge of foreign languages for the Ph.D.

There are not many fields of academic studies where knowledge of languages is as indispensable as in musicology. I will pass over the Slavic or the Asiatic or African languages, which may be regarded as a matter for specialized studies, and I will leave aside Greek and Spanish, desirable as they may be. But in any case at least five languages are indispensable to the study of the history of Western music—that is, Latin, English, French, Italian, and German.[9]

IOWA: German, French, and one other language (usually Latin or Italian) before taking comprehensives. NC: Departmental examinations in 2 modern foreign languages. CLAREMONT: German and French, Italian, or Latin. INDIANA: French by the end of "one calendar year following enrollment" in addition to the German that was required for the master's degree, plus "a third foreign language (if required by the student's dissertation advisor) by the end of six terms of residence." PRINCETON: German and either French or Italian. "Students must complete the language requirements before taking the general examination. The department recommends, however, that one language examination be passed during the first year. Preference in admission will be given to applicants who show that they are already qualified in this respect. Entering students should, if necessary, begin to prepare themselves for these examinations in the months preceding the first term of graduate study." MICHIGAN: In historical musicology, 2 languages, basic level, one of which must be German; in ethnomusicology, French and German, basic level, or one of these plus a thesis-related language. (See MICHIGAN'S warning, pages 59–60, about the need to study languages before arriving on campus.) HARVARD: German and either French or Italian before taking the general examination; a third language "appropriate to the field of specialization" must be passed "after completing the General Exam and within one year of the approval of a dissertation

---

[9]Friedrich Blume in *Perspectives in Musicology*, op.cit., p. 18.

proposal." TORONTO: See page 69. NYU (historical musicology): German and either French or Italian. The first examination, preferably in German, must be taken during the first semester of graduate study, and the second before the end of the third term of full-time study. NYU (ethnomusicology): As above for historical musicology, except that some other foreign language may be substituted for French or Italian, subject to the approval of the ethnomusicology coordinator. WESLEYAN: "The candidate may be required to study languages appropriate to his or her area of specialization."

YALE: German plus 2 of these 3: French, Latin, Italian. No permission to take the qualifying examination until all foreign language examinations are passed. "Since reading assignments in foreign languages are an integral part of the course work, students are urged to master the required languages as soon as possible." WISCONSIN: In music history, 2 foreign languages, one of which must be German; in ethnomusicology, French and German; "other foreign languages may also be required depending on the student's geographical area of specialization." "All language requirements should be fulfilled by the end of the student's second semester in residence." MARYLAND: In musicology, German and "at least one other pertinent foreign language"; in ethnomusicology, German or French and an appropriate field language. Reading-knowledge tests must be passed "either upon entrance to the program or within one semester of enrollment for the first language and two semesters of enrollment for the second." CUNY GRADUATE CENTER: 2 language examinations, usually in German and French. ILLINOIS: German and at least one other language, "depending on the proposed field of specialization. This requirement can be satisfied by evidence of two years of undergraduate study, by completion of a two-semester reading course with a grade of at least B, or by satisfactory test scores."

UT AT AUSTIN: German and French before being allowed to take the qualifying examination; any substitute language requires special approval. A third language is expected if the student's specialty needs it. UNT: Usually French and German, demonstrated through a local reading test (as follow-up of a special course in the language department), or through the Graduate Student Foreign Language Test, or through at least a B average in 4 semesters of a course, with the last semester having been taken within 3 years of the qualifying examination. PENN: German, either French or Italian, and a third foreign language. "Students may petition to substitute for the third language a special skill that has a significant bearing on their advanced research." BERKELEY:

In historical musicology, French, German, and liturgical Latin; option to replace Latin with a suitable substitute. In ethnomusicology, German, the language of the specialty, and a third language "in which appreciable research in the special field has been published." STANFORD: "German and either French or Italian and any other language necessary to research in the candidate's field of specialization." CHICAGO: "A reading knowledge of three foreign languages: German, Latin, and French or Italian. Under special circumstances, substitutions will be considered by individual petition to the Department. Students will not be admitted to doctoral seminars until the relevant language requirements are completed."

Evaluations, general examinations, candidacy for the Ph.D.

ALL: General examinations may be repeated, some say once, some say twice.

STANFORD: A qualifying examination in the second year and "a later comprehensive written exam in the candidate's special area of concentration . . . plus the University Oral."

CUNY GRADUATE CENTER: A written first examination on reaching 30 credits; this serves as a qualifying examination for the final 30 credits and entitles the student to the "en route" M.A., which is awarded at 45 credits. A second (or comprehensive) examination on completion of all course work.

MICHIGAN (historical musicology): General preliminary and field examinations during the fourth term of residence, both of which are in the primary areas. The general preliminary examination is written, and deals with "all the musical genres from a given period." The field examination is oral, on a particular area within the principal field of study; it is related to the dissertation topic, but broader. The academic advisor and the student confer beforehand to define the boundaries of both examinations. Doctoral candidacy is conferred when the program of study, language examinations, theory preliminary examination, and general preliminary examination are successfully completed; the dissertation committee is selected when the field examination is successfully completed.

MICHIGAN (ethnomusicology): 3 written preliminary examinations and an oral examination before the conferral of doctoral candidacy: 1) general preliminary in Western music history, 2) general preliminary in

Western music theory, 3) preliminary in ethnomusicology, 4) oral on the proposed dissertation and the student's qualifications to pursue it successfully.

An alternative plan if the doctoral student in ethnomusicology is Asian or African and plans to return to his or her home country: 1) general preliminary in the music of the student's country or region; 2) preliminary in ethnomusicology; 3) either a general preliminary in Western music history, a general preliminary in Western music theory, or a preliminary in anthropology, linguistics, or the history of the student's country or region (the latter to be administered by the appropriate department); 4) oral on the proposed dissertation and the student's qualifications to pursue it successfully. "This option is subject to the approval of the Department of Music History and Musicology and any other department involved, and the home institution of the student. A student approved for this option must nevertheless complete a course sequence in Western music with a grade of B or higher in each course." This is the course sequence: introduction to graduate study; 2 courses in music history, one of which emphasizes repertoire; 5 courses in undergraduate and upper-division theory "unless this requirement is waived through the theory placement examination."

INDIANA: To qualify for doctoral candidacy, a written examination on the content of courses as well as on "background, concepts, and ideologies"; a written examination based on identifying examples of music; and an oral examination.

YALE: "To continue pursuit of the Ph.D. degree, a student must be admitted to candidacy by vote of the faculty of the Department. This normally occurs at the end of a student's second year. Admission to candidacy is granted if the student has received a grade of Honors in two full-year courses or in four term courses and has produced work of a quality that demonstrates adequate preparation for passing the qualifying examination and writing a satisfactory dissertation. A student who has not been admitted to candidacy will not be permitted to register for the third year."

The qualifying examination is normally taken at the beginning of the third year; it may come earlier or later with faculty approval. For the Ph.D. in music history it consists of 1) a 2-hour closed-book essay on each of 4 pairs of musical examples from all historical periods (total, 8 hours); 2) a one-day historical, theoretical, and analytical evaluation of a single composition (chosen from 3), using all the resources of the university libraries; and 3) a 2-hour oral examination on the pieces selected in the first 2 parts of the examination.

NYU: The qualifying examination comes at the end of the term in which 36 points of graduate courses are completed. On general knowledge of music history and theory. Preparation should include independent reading as well as coursework. Students who have to repeat the examination may register only provisionally until it is passed.

"A student who passes the qualifying examination may proceed with coursework and may take a special examination in the field of specialization, administered by his or her dissertation committee within a year of the qualifying examination."

WISCONSIN: "The preliminary examination must be passed no later than the end of the second complete year of residence after the master's degree. The purpose of this policy is to move successful candidates promptly to more advanced and specialized research work, including the dissertation. . . .

"Preliminary examinations may be taken only after foreign language requirements and required course work in music and the minor area have been completed, and removal of any deficiencies. Examinations will be both written and oral. The written examination will be in the student's area of specialization, the general history of music, and the general theory of music. The oral examination is taken following successful completion of the written examination and upon recommendation of the student's adviser and approval by the Director of Graduate Studies." The content of the oral examination depends partly on the results of the written.

WEST VIRGINIA: "Completion of course work does not guarantee success on the comprehensive examination."

NC: "Following the completion of course work and language requirements, Ph.D. students will take a written examination in three areas of specialization to be determined through consultation with the faculty, and an oral examination focused largely on the area of the proposed dissertation."

HARVARD: "The progress of all graduate students is reviewed at the end of each year. In addition to adequate course work, there are special requirements for first and second year students. Every student must submit at least one paper written for a graduate course as part of the first year review. Musicology students must take an analysis exam. . . ."

The General Examination, taken at the end of the second year, has 2 parts, written and oral. The oral comes 1–2 weeks after passing the written. The written part is administered in 4 sections over 2 days: history and literature, analysis, "and a special field of non-Western music chosen by the student and submitted to the Graduate Advisor in writing at least two months before the Examination." The oral is based partly on the results of the written. The general examination is "not necessarily related to topics covered in seminars."

UT AT AUSTIN: "A student taking the candidacy exams should demonstrate a competent knowledge of the general history of music as well as a more extensive knowledge of two specific fields or subjects (usually defined as musical eras or topics of a systematic nature). One of these, which includes within it the student's dissertation topic, will be considered the principal area; the other, the secondary area, and both fields must be approved by the faculty of the Musicology Division at least four months prior to the scheduled examinations. For each of the chosen areas the student will be expected to show a firm grasp of its music history and literature, bibliography, historiography, methods and problems, and cultural context."

PENN: As noted above, "A written comprehensive examination in the history and theory of music serves as both the final examination for the A.M. degree and the preliminary examination for doctoral candidacy."

"Doctoral candidates take an oral special field examination in the broad area in which the dissertation will be written."

TORONTO: See page 69.

ILLINOIS: "A preliminary examination is taken after all course work is completed."

BERKELEY: Admission to doctoral candidacy requires not only that the qualifying examination be passed but that the dissertation topic be approved. The qualifying examination "may be scheduled at any time in the academic year, typically at the end of the student's second year in the doctoral program. An examining committee of five faculty members, one from outside the Department of Music, is nominated by the Graduate Adviser in consultation with the candidate. . . ."

In historical musicology, written and oral parts. "The written part requires evidence of the candidate's ability in writing and research independent of regular course work. This requirement will normally be satisfied by the dissertation prospectus. . . . In some circumstances, however, the Graduate Committee may accept in place of the prospectus a published paper (or one that it has accepted or deemed suitable for publication), or may assign the candidate a short research project to be completed in one week.

"The oral part (three hours) takes place about three weeks after the successful completion of the written part. It covers three topics:

"1. The first two topics should cover the history and literature of two periods of music history such as the following: antiquity to plain chant and early polyphony to Perotin; medieval polyphony from Perotin to Ars subtilior and Dufay-Palestrina; the Classic period and Romanticism through Wagner; Verdi to World War II and World War II to the present.

"2. The works of a major composer from a historical area not covered by the chosen period. The composer must be one with a substantial output, which has been treated extensively in the literature. The candidate is expected to show a knowledge of the relevant sources and bibliography, as well as the critical and analytical approaches appropriate to the composer's style."

In ethnomusicology, also written and oral parts. The written part is the same as for historical musicology. "The oral part takes place about three weeks after the successful completion of the written part. It covers three topics:

"1. The music of a geographic area such as the following: India, Indonesia, Japan, China, South America, North America, Europe.

"2. Either a.) the music of a second geographic area or b.) literature on a particular approach, theory, or focus in ethnomusicology such as the following: Organology, linguistic studies, etc.

"3. Cultural studies pertinent to topics one and two."

CHICAGO: Two examinations. The first is a "qualifying examination to test the candidate's general knowledge of the history and theory of music. For students taking their M.A. degree at the University of Chicago, this examination is the same as the M.A. examination . . . [see pages 62–63], which is normally taken at the end of Scholastic Residence [the period devoted primarily to course work]. Students entering the Ph.D. program with a Master's degree from another university are required to take the qualifying examination at the end of one year of Scholastic Residence. (In exceptional circumstances and upon petition to the Department the examination may be postponed by one quarter.)"

The second is a "special field examination to test the student's knowledge of a two-hundred-year period that will normally encompass the research area of the student's dissertation topic. The normal format of the special field examination is as follows:

"1. Two major written essays each taking approximately one and a half hours. The student is usually given a choice of two out of three questions.

"2. A number of short essays each taking approximately thirty to forty-five minutes. The student is usually given a choice of three out of five questions.

"3. A series of brief identifications (typically 25 terms, names, titles, etc., to be identified in an hour).

"The student is usually given one full day (9:00 a.m. to 4:30 p.m.) to complete this examination."

UNT: "The purpose of the Qualifying Examination is to establish the student's status as a candidate for the degree by measuring accomplishment and knowledge of the art of music as a whole. The examination covers all fields of music study, with particular emphasis on the student's major field. The exam may not be taken until the language and keyboard requirements are satisfied, and all course deficiencies have been removed, and after completion of most of the course work."

In musicology, 2 long essays and 6 short essays on subjects selected from music history; identification of 20 examples of music; identification of 20 musical terms, titles, or names of composers; analysis, with score and recording, of a selected composition; analysis of three works or sections in score, from the medieval or Renaissance, Classic or Romantic, and modern periods; composition of a 3- or 4-voice section of music.

IOWA: The dissertation topic must be approved before the comprehensive examination is taken. The examination is "either written or oral or both. The committee for the comprehensive examination shall consist of three faculty members from musicology and two from other areas in the School of Music."

MARYLAND: "The two-day [written] examinations assess student mastery in the area of specialization and in the broad field of music.... An oral examination may additionally be scheduled at the discretion of the Graduate Adviser and the faculty in the area of specialization."

PRINCETON: "Before taking the general examination, every student is expected to have developed wide acquaintance with music and writing about music, over and above the course requirements, and to have competed as an essential part of his or her program a specific piece of research. . . .

". . .the general examination has no necessary relation to courses in the graduate curriculum but is without limitation as to the nature of the questions asked, within the field of musicology as tempered by current issues and interests.

"A student with a strong focus and demonstrated competence in . . . comparative musicology may have a specially designed general examination.

"Students who have sustained the general examination are qualified to receive the degree of master of fine arts. Further studies leading to the degree of doctor of philosophy are offered for those students who have shown distinction in their work. For this degree [in musicology], the further requirements are a dissertation . . . and a final public oral examination."

UBC: Written and oral, covering three of the traditional historical periods, and with a theory and analysis component consisting of the "General Comprehensive Examination in music theory."

Dissertation

ALL: An oral examination upon completion of the dissertation.

MOST: While it is assumed that the graduate school will impose the requirement of writing an abstract for *Dissertation Abstracts*, only a few program descriptions formally call for an abstract for RILM and the early registration of topics with *Doctoral Dissertations in Musicology*.

STANFORD: "The Ph.D. candidate must submit a dissertation that demonstrates his or her capacity for independent advanced research. . . . The dissertation is principally a test of scholarly method and clear exposition, with an emphasis upon quality of work rather than scope or length."

NC: As noted on page 85, part of the general examination is "an oral examination focused largely on the area of the proposed dissertation."

CHICAGO: "Within one month after having passed the special field examination each candidate should submit a formal dissertation proposal, written in consultation with a faculty advisor of the student's choice. The student and faculty advisor will consult on the selection of one or more additional faculty members who will be asked to serve on the dissertation committee. The proposal must demonstrate the propriety and feasibility of the topic and the student's knowledge of the existing literature about it. A bibliography must be appended to the proposal. When the proposal is accepted by the dissertation committee it will then be filed in the student's dossier in the Department of Music. Changes in the topic must be submitted to the dissertation committee....

"Admission to candidacy. After the successful completion of the examinations described above and the submission of the proposal, the student will be recommended by the Department of Music to the Dean of Students for admission to candidacy for the Ph.D. degree. At least nine months (three quarters) must normally elapse between admission to candidacy and the final examination [defense of the dissertation]....

"Normally, attainment of the M.A. degree, whether at the university of Chicago or elsewhere, or its equivalent, is a precondition to admission to candidacy. Note that it is University policy that students cannot be admitted to candidacy until they have passed their special field examination, have passed all required language examinations, and have received acceptance by their Department of a formal dissertation proposal submitted by the student. Further, in the Department of Music dissertation defenses will not be scheduled until candidates have passed all practicum examinations and have made up all incomplete work.

"[The dissertation must make] an original contribution to knowledge. The dissertation must be approved by at least two members of the Department who can verify that it meets the necessary requirements. The dissertation should normally be completed within three years after the special field examination. However, the student may petition the Department for yearly extensions.

"There is a final oral examination in defense of the dissertation."

YALE: "Within three months after passing the Ph.D. qualifying examination, the student will submit a dissertation prospectus to the Director of Graduate Studies. Such a prospectus will outline the nature and scope of the topic and will offer a tentative title for the dissertation. Upon receiving the material, the DGS will study it and arrange for its review by a committee chaired by a permanent member of the faculty, and including the DGS, ex officio, and any other faculty the DGS may deem appropriate. After the prospectus committee has met with the student, it will formulate a verbal or written report for the DGS. This report will include a formal response to the prospectus, recommending its acceptance, rejection, or acceptance contingent on revision. If the prospectus is rejected the student will reformulate the material and then meet again with the committee. Once a prospectus has been approved in its final state, a copy will be submitted to the registrar of the Graduate School and the original will be kept at the Department. Any substantive change of title or scope of the dissertation must be submitted for approval by the committee. . . .a student may also transmit a written or oral request that a particular advisor be assigned for the dissertation . . . [and] every attempt will be made to comply with that request. . . ."

BERKELEY: "Students are urged to find their particular fields of research as early as possible in their graduate careers, usually by means of advanced seminars in the chosen areas of study and by [special-studies] courses investigating possibilities opened up during the seminars.

"Then in consultation with a member of the faculty, the candidate will write up proposals for the project in the form of a prospectus. It should generally be presented for approval before the oral qualifying examination, but in no circumstances may it be submitted later than a semester after the examination. . . .

"The Graduate Committee keeps a Progress Chart on which the [dissertation] supervisor indicates the work that has been accomplished in each semester. . . ." If a dissertation in historical musicology has not been completed 2 years after admission to candidacy (3 years for ethnomusicology), "the Graduate Committee will conduct a formal review of the student's progress in conjunction with the student and the supervisor."

MICHIGAN (historical musicology and ethnomusicology): "Each Ph.D. candidate will present, in a public forum before an audience of students and departmental faculty, a proposal outlining the topic, methodology, and results of his or her dissertation research to date. The proposal will take the form of a written paper and will be circulated in advance to a faculty member who will offer suggestions and comments after the candidate's presentation. Copies should also be placed in the Music Library for others to read before the public presentation. The proposal will customarily be presented at a point when the candidate can benefit most from the exchange: after enough research has taken place to define the chief issues of the topic but before a large portion has been written. In any event, the presentation should take place within the first year of candidacy."

MARYLAND: "A minimum of twelve semester credit hours in dissertation research . . . must be earned. The topic of the dissertation is selected and proposed by the student and approved by the Department of Music. . . . The dissertation may deal with any aspect of music. It must be formal, systematic, original, and written in clear, correct English."

NYU: As noted above, a special examination is given the student who has passed the qualifying examination. The special examination is in the student's field of emphasis; it is "administered by his future dissertation committee and taken within a year of the qualifying examination. When the student has qualified for official candidacy, a committee is appointed for advisement, consisting of a principal reader and two other faculty advisers."

TORONTO: See page 69.

COLORADO, WASHINGTON: As noted on page 71, the same number of credits are assigned to the dissertation as are assigned to Ph.D. coursework beyond the master's degree.

HARVARD: "The third year is primarily devoted to developing a dissertation proposal and the beginning of work on the dissertation. All students will take at least two more half courses, the topics of which may be assigned by the faculty as a result of the General Examination. Musicology students must complete the third language. . . . A public colloquium must be given on a topic of the student's choice, which may be related to the work in progress on the dissertation. . . .

"Within one year after completion of the General Examinations, the Ph.D. candidate is expected to develop a proposal for a dissertation, which should be a major original contribution to the field. The proposal must be submitted for approval to the Department, which is responsible for assigning the student committee consisting of a dissertation advisor and two other faculty members. Normally, the complete dissertation must be submitted within five years after passing the General Examination, and satisfactory progress must be demonstrated every year in order that the student remain in good standing. . . . A public colloquium on the dissertation is required after it has been completed and approved."

UNT: The dissertation topic "must be approved by the Ph.D. Committee . . . after the candidate has successfully completed the Qualifying Examination." At the final oral examination the candidate is questioned not only on such dissertation topics as relevant bibliography and sources in foreign languages, but also on music literature in general: "the principal classes in chamber music; orchestral; piano; and vocal repertoires, including solo, opera, oratorio, and choral music. . . ."

IOWA: Like the M.A. thesis topic, the Ph.D. thesis topic must first be informally approved by the faculty; then a formal and detailed proposal is written.

COLUMBIA: See the note about Columbia's M. Phil. program (page 65). "After receiving the M. Phil. degree, students, according to the recommendation of the department, either write a dissertation under the sponsorship of a faculty member or satisfy the requirements *extra muros*."

WESLEYAN: "Although most dissertations are expository, written documents, the department recognizes the possibility of a variety of formats and media, limited only by the stipulation that the work take a form which allows it to be presented, preserved and studied."

CONCLUSIONS: WHERE WE ARE NOW

Our basic goals have not changed much since mid-century

The essential shape of American musicology as it became more or less established by the fifties and sixties is still intact as the century comes to an end, if university curricula are any indication. A visitor from one university's musicological territory will not feel seriously out of place on other campuses. And where there are important differences in curricula, these lie not so much in different value judgments as they do in different degrees of emphasis and different modes of operation.

Is this apparent stability owing to mere inertia rather than trial and error and hard-won conviction? Is it now eroding at an accelerating rate? If so, is most of the erosion being caused by the most powerful social force of our time—namely, the ambition to foster or restore individual cultural, ethnic, and political identities? Is it inevitable that no widely sanctioned curriculum in the humanities, no canon, can maintain its central importance while one group after another clamors to have its own rights and its own contributions recognized? Or is it more important than ever to hang on to the (pardon a hackneyed and preposterous term) eternal verities that have made Western society the envy of most of the rest of the world?

It may be that the first wave of what is derogatorily and unfairly called "political correctness" has receded from American campuses. A central theme in the 1991 meeting of the Modern Language Association was that the literary classics are being enriched and broadened, not replaced, by the more open outlook of American academia.[1] Most of the papers read at the annual meetings of the American Musicological Society in the early nineties fell far short of establishing a new musicological paradigm; where they actually fell was back into the traditional compartments of historical musicology, as if in reaction to the 1990 meeting's vast panorama of gender-race-class-folk-pop-rock-semiotics-new criticism-ethnology. In 1990, of course, the AMS met jointly with the Society for Ethnomusicology and the Society for Music Theory. That obvious explanation may or may not be enough to account for the striking difference in tone. But around the campus in the first half of the nineties the terrain does indeed look very much like it always has; the creations of dead white males are, for the moment, only being supplemented (enriched, cheapened, reinforced, diluted, broadened, narrowed) rather than being extensively replaced by the products of alternate value systems. The postmodernist debates that one finds these

[1]*Washington Post*, Jan. 3, 1992.

days in the e-mail of young musicologists have not yet caused any seismic disturbances.

Perhaps we should look for trends toward or away from alternate value systems only in the programs of the next *several joint meetings* of AMS, SEM, and SMT.

We want our new graduate students to arrive with a strong background in performance and general musicianship

The old ideal of Randall Thompson and Manfred Bukofzer, that of producing enlightened musical amateurs only in the college or university and professional performers only in the conservatory, is all but dead in America. In the same way that the practical necessities of vocational education have invaded the empyrean sphere of classical studies in all the humanities, university training in practical musicianship—at a high if not professional level—has become not merely the sine qua non of true musical understanding but an end in itself. That is a large part of the background of INDIANA'S or IOWA'S performance prerequisite for graduate studies in musicology. Bukofzer would be more satisfied with NYU or COLUMBIA or BERKELEY, where competent performance is, for scholars, an avenue to understanding, and, theoretically at least, nothing more. Thompson would be disappointed to learn that at the undergraduate level most music majors, including those destined for graduate study in musicology, must now aspire to the highest performance level they can achieve, even if it means neglecting literature, languages, science, history, philosophy.

Therefore, when the new crop of graduate students arrives, we make the most of their better-than-European practical musicianship and try to get along as best we can with their worse-than-European training in the liberal arts. They may or may not particularly need further training in practical musicianship, such as CHICAGO'S series of practicum examinations, but it is a dead certainty that:

The vast majority of our new graduate students will be poorly trained in the liberal arts, especially foreign languages

The main message of all undergraduate music curricula endorsed by the National Association of Schools of Music is that the student must be trained first as a practical musician. Liberal arts are required, but they are second in importance. If an undergraduate already happens to be an accomplished practical musician and wishes now to set perform-ance aside in order to take more courses in such subjects as foreign languages and history, NASM makes it very difficult for him or her to do so, as long as the university wants to keep its NASM accreditation. Such conflicts between musical professionalism and undergraduate liberal-arts training are the main cause of the administrative separation of "college" and "conservatory" at some institutions. YALE, for instance, has a School of Music for practical musicians, and Department of Music for scholars. There seems to be no good reason why performers and scholars cannot be productively "thrown together," as Gustave Reese put it, under such a plan of organization; and there are plenty of reasons why such a plan might offer the academically gifted a long head start in musicology.

As it is, a great gulf separates most newly minted American Bach-elors of Arts and Bachelors of Music from the discipline of musicology. They lack imagination because they have hardly ever contemplated the thrilling possibilities of a world beyond the practice room. They cannot write because they have seldom been asked to marshal their thoughts in writing. They remain ignorant of the most fundamental literature of musicology for the amazing reason that they can read only English. Their knowledge of history and of historical style periods is so fragmen-tary that they can commonly be off by two hundred years in identifying a musical excerpt. If they survive the rigors of the graduate musicology curriculum, they begin their careers in a narrow niche of musicology and pursue those careers by becoming narrower. Only liberal education can cure these ills.

Having said all that (twice now in this document), I add the obvious corollary statement: Graduate training in musicology would make a quantum leap ahead if *undergraduate* curricula in music were properly overhauled to make more room for that rare undergraduate who is gifted as both musician and scholar.